I0816165

William F. Buckley Jr.'s Guide to Friendship in a Polarized Era

Lessons in Civility from a Catholic Conservative Icon

Josh Cohen

FIDELIS PUBLISHING®

ISBN: 9781956454925
ISBN (eBook): 9781956454932

William F. Buckley Jr.'s Guide to Friendship in a Polarized Era: Lessons in Civility from a Catholic Conservative Icon

Cover Design by Diana Lawrence
Interior Design by Xcel Graphic
Edited by Lisa Guest

Order at www.faithfultext.com for a significant discount. Email info@fidelis publishing.com to inquire about bulk purchase discounts.

Fidelis Publishing, LLC • Winchester, VA / Nashville, TN •
fidelispublishing.com

Manufactured in the United States of America

10 9 8 7 6 5 4 3 2 1

Buckley was a "genius at friendships that surpass all understanding."

—Liberal Journalist Murray Kempton on William F. Buckley Jr.

For J. Randy Taraborelli,

best-selling author, multiple-time interviewee,
friend, and mentor,

without whom this book and the accompanying
words

would still be sheltered in the halls of my knotted
mind

CONTENTS

FOREWORD

LtCol Oliver North, USMC (Ret)

In these times of bitter, divisive political discourse, thoughtful, reasonable words are oft drowned out by the cacophony of twisted "social media;" perversions proffered as edification by educators; and distorted rants by "experts" shouting on "podcasts" and in the so-called "main-stream media." For these reasons, and many more, Josh Cohen's new book, *William F. Buckley, Jr.'s Guide to Friendship in a Polarized Era: Lessons in Civility* is a must read for those of us who care about the future of our nation, our children, and grandchildren.

During my youth, Bill Buckley was widely regarded as one of the most influential figures in American politics and conservative morality. He certainly was for me. While still in high school, I read his first book, *God and Man at Yale* (1951); devoured every copy of *National Review* I could find (founded by Buckley in 1955); and must confess to have watched every possible episode of *Firing Line* on PBS (more than 1,400 broadcasts from 1966 to 1999).

Full disclosure also requires me to admit it was Bill Buckley who gave me my first "break" in television—and in the event—validated Cohen's claims about Buckley's legendary civility.

In the summer of 1971, Seymour Hersh came out with a book in which he suggested war crimes were commonplace in Vietnam. Buckley invited him to appear on *Firing Line* prompting Marine Captains John Bender, Don Carpenter, and me to write a letter to Mr. Buckley expressing our outrage at Hersh's insinuations.

Not only did Buckley reply, he also invited us to appear on his show to discuss the issue. His letter to Colonel Bill Davis, our Commanding Officer at The Basic School—where we were training new Marine officers—was sent to the Commanding General who in turn forwarded it to Marine Headquarters in Washington where a public affairs officer replied, "Okay why not?"

On June 7, 1979, we taped the show at American University in Washington before a live audience. I was struck by Buckley's posture. He slouched so badly I thought he was about to fall off his chair. Marine officers who have served in combat generally don't get nervous about speaking in public but to be interviewed by William F. Buckley Jr. was more than a little intimidating. Should I bring along a dictionary? Unlike Buckley (Yale), Bender (Princeton) and Carpenter (Brown)—all Ivy League grads—I attended a "trade school," the U.S. Naval Academy in Annapolis, MD. I was uncertain I would comprehend the copious, elongated, locutions Mr. Buckley was inclined to employ. In the end, I managed to understand most of his vocabulary and all his questions.

On the air, the three of us explained it would be a terrible injustice if everyone who served in Vietnam returned home—dead or alive—under suspicion of being a war criminal. We did not suggest war crimes never occurred. But all three of us served in combat and none of us even heard anything like Hersch alleged until we came home. To the contrary, we gave eye-witness testimony to the care taken by our Marines to avoid endangering innocent lives. The rules of engagement were so strict, there were times our men were in greater danger and in some cases cost American lives.

In the 1980's, during certain televised Congressional hearings, Mr. Buckley sent me several encouraging notes. Since then, I have been interviewed thousands of times by thousands of interviewers and Bill Buckley stands out in my mind as among the very best. He combined thorough preparation, intellect, and pursuit for truth, not headlines, to asking Seymour Hersh and three tough Marines, hard questions with civility.

Josh Cohen also eloquently captures another "Buckley Virtue" in this book—his persistent quest to expose intellectual corrosion and anti-Christian corruption in America's academic institutions. Cohen kindly cites U.S. Marine co-authors David Goetsch, Archie Jones, and me in our book, *American Gulags* in which we wrote, ". . . when [one] examines[s] the unaltered historical record, what becomes undeniably clear is that the United States of America was founded by Christians and built on a solid foundation of biblical principles and Christian values."

Though I never asked him, Bill Buckley certainly knew from his study of Latin:

"Semper Fidelis" is more than a slogan for U.S. Marines.
"Always Faithful" is a way of life

CHAPTER 1

Faith and Friendship: The Dual Pillars of William F. Buckley Jr.

It seems almost breathtakingly ironic that William F. Buckley Jr.—perhaps the single most consequential conservative in American history—might be the ideal figure to look to for lessons on friendship that cheerfully bridges ideological divides. Buckley, who lived many lives in print and television as a polemicist and picked open fights with numerous institutions and establishments, nonetheless embodied values transcending partisanship. His life and the way he practiced his faith-informed values offer an inspiring model in today's hypertribal landscape.

When he was at Yale, a professor took him to one side and asked Buckley to broaden his horizons and take a class in metaphysics. Buckley replied, "I have God and my father. That's all I need."[97]

John Fink, editor emeritus of *The Criterion* with the Archdiocese of Indianapolis, wrote, Buckley "was undoubtedly the most important U.S. Catholic political conservative during the second half of the 20th century."[1] That doesn't really run the risk of being much of an exaggeration.

His ability to maintain meaningful friendships with those who held diametrically opposed views was not merely a testament to his personal charm and wit (though there was that) but also to his profound understanding and appreciation of Catholic teachings on love, respect, and the inherent dignity of each individual.

Buckley was a man on a mission "preaching the demands of the Church in the secular realm" through his considerable literary output, including the celebrated polemic *God and Man at Yale: The Superstitions of Academic Freedom*, which, among other things, criticized the virulent outbreak of secularism that had infiltrated Yale; the prestigious conservative organ *National Review*; and, of course, his television program *Firing Line*.[2]

Buckley's son, Christopher, author of, among many other books, the celebrated satire *Thank You for Smoking*, said of his father, "His faith was the molten core of his being, and I think you could extrapolate from that everything about my father."[2] And it is Buckley's faith that sustained, inspired, and guided him to the measured heights and considerable cultural and political influence he achieved throughout his remarkable life.

Buckley would certainly have noticed the emaciation of Christian ideals in today's society. This emaciation fed into the universities, media, journalism, and so on, causing a general destabilization of what we would regard as truth. But more on that later.

Rich Lowry, the current editor-in-chief of *National Review* who was handpicked by Buckley to man the helm, marveled at how Buckley's faith was "absolutely foundational" and he never had "any hint of doubt" about his faith, reaching heights of certainty most can never dream of even attaining.[5]

"Buckley certainly wanted a Christian culture," Lowry revealed to me, "and was worried about its erosion in the 1950s, so he would be even more shocked by where it is today."

Lowry went on to relate, while Buckley's firm thoughts on the matter would no doubt be nuanced and idiosyncratic, he would generally agree with the idea of reinstating Christian principles in public life.

Buckley sharpened the point in a 1997 interview where he asserted the "ubiquity" and "universally informative" utility of the Christian ideal.[3]

He would certainly prescribe, as the antidote to so much of the current cultural destabilization, an orientation toward Christianity.

The need for lessons in Christianity are "accentuated by the extent to which they are not heeded," Buckley warned in that same interview, with worrying prescience.[3]

So many societal and cultural ills, Buckley thought—crime, a lack of concern for one's fellow man, and no doubt he would include a number of other ills to the list were he alive today—Christianity can aid in the pursuit of understanding and answers to that kind of phenomena.

This is by no means to suggest Buckley was in any way a pacifist, as may often be thought of the highly religious. His support of the Vietnam War alone would test that, certainly his own time in the army as well. But, regarding today's society, Buckley would have fought against the moral anesthesia pacifism so often induces.

For pacifism is simply a cowardly way of allowing evil to penetrate the culture and proliferate in the world while simultaneously congratulating yourself for having so passively aided in that moral breach.

Buckley's faith was such that it would demand action in the eternal struggle against evil.

Buckley's theological fealty to Catholicism extended further in commitment than many popes! I know that sounds like hyperbole, but here it isn't. Buckley was certainly more Catholic in preaching and practice than was Pope Francis.

Buckley took umbrage with a few of the reformations made to the Holy See as a result of the Second Vatican Council, which took place from 1962 to 1965.

His son, Christopher, again takes up the mantle for his father by commenting, "Pup was a defiantly pre-Vatican II Catholic" to the point that he had a priest say "a private Latin mass for him" every Sunday[4]. This meant he, to make a long story short (which may be too late), shirked the Vatican II reform encouraging the use of vernacular languages in the Mass to promote active participation and accessibility for the laity (those who were not priests, nuns, bishops, etc.).

Whatever one wants to call that, either in praise or critique, they cannot call it a lack of devotion.

Conservative historian and *National Review* contributor Matthew Continetti adds, "That devotion ends up being kind of at the core of Buckley's understanding of what love is. Love of one's friends, one's family and one's country."[6]

Buckley once wrote, "Our burden is to keep the faith."[7] Buckley, as with all mortals of the temporal world, could only graze on the lower slopes of knowledge and understanding of the cosmos and God's plan for it, but he tried his best.

He went on to write, "The greatest tonic of all is divine love, which is nourished by human love, even as human love is nourished by divine love."[7]

It was upon this apparent paradox Buckley took his philosophical stances.

"To ponder the glory of God," Buckley explained, "is to worship a transcendence that gives us a measure of man, near-infinitely small on the scale of things, but infinitely great, as the complement of divine love. Who are you, buster? *I am the man Christ-God died for.*"[7]

He seemed to exemplify that age-old adage of not being a human being having a spiritual experience but of existing as a spiritual being having a human experience and that the temporal world is but a long vale of tears which we shall all eventually pass through.

The former mayoral candidate of New York, Buckley wrote, it is mostly features of the material world from which we as human beings derive our satisfactions:

> The love of our family, the company of our friends, the feel of the wind on the face, the excitement of the printed page, the delights of color and form and sounds; food, wine, sex. But there is that other life that only human beings experience, and in that life, and from that life, other pulsations are felt. They press upon us, in the Christian vision, one thing again and again, which is that God loves us. The best way to put it is that God would give His life for us and, in Christ, did.[7]

Buckley cited Christ directly on this point. Christ was asked which is the greatest commandment, most begging to be heeded. Christ's answer included the second commandment: "Thou shalt love thy neighbor as thyself" (Matthew 22:39). [Bible 1]

In an effort to further consecrate himself to the faith of which he was such a devout follower, Buckley sought, in 1994, to make a pilgrimage to the legendary Marion city of Lourdes in France where supposedly God's healing hand has been evident for centuries.

Because God does have a sense of humor (simply look at the platypus), Buckley—the celebrated spy novelist—first made a somewhat shorter pilgrimage to his doctor's office the day prior to his flight. Buckley's incessant labor, as Christopher Hitchens would later call it, had taken enough of a toll on the tireless workhorse he was being fairly brutally punished by his refractory sense. This was after a particularly grueling lecture tour, which demanded he board an airplane for twenty-one consecutive days.

His doctor told him to come back the following day for sinus X-rays. Buckley said that wasn't doable as he had, of course, to board a plane the next day. Perhaps there was a mild challenge to his faith when he wrote he simply couldn't believe Our Lady would curse him with a malady prior to leaving for Lourdes.

Buckley and his doc struck a deal that he would go, straightaway, to get the scans that day. Upon the proper examination, he may get the green light to make his flight to the holy Catholic city.

The doctor's assistant later said, according to Buckley, "The doctor said since you're going to go anyway, we may as well let you go."[7]

So, off Buckley went along with his sister Priscilla who, by the way, was managing editor for *National Review*. Armed with the expected arsenal of antibiotics and sleeping pills despite traveling to the city regarded for its relationship with the divine powers of convalescence, Buckley might have suspected the irony strained the natural serendipity of coincidence.

Lourdes is located in the foothills of the Pyrenees mountains. Legend states it was once the object of avarice of the famed conqueror Charlemagne in the 18th century. It is one of the most significant pilgrimage sites in the Catholic world due to reported apparitions of the Virgin Mary that occurred there in 1858. A young peasant girl named Bernadette Soubirous claimed to have seen the Virgin Mary, also referred to as the Lady in White, in no fewer than eighteen separate visions near a grotto, now called the Grotto of Massabielle. Soubirous's recounting of these apparitions, which is recounted by Buckley in some detail, were "always direct and unambiguous."[7]

Since these apparitions, Lourdes has become a major destination for those seeking healing. The spring water from the grotto is believed by many to have miraculous properties, and millions of pilgrims visit the town each year, often bathing in the waters with the hope of experiencing physical or spiritual healing. The Sanctuary of Our Lady of Lourdes, which includes the grotto, basilicas, and various chapels, is the central site of religious activity in the town.

The small French town has captivated believers and skeptics for centuries since. Buckley asserted, not admitted, even the ardent Christian doesn't really know what goes on at Lourdes because they are unable to reason why some of its visitors see relief or cure when others don't. He was, however, quick to point out that while the nonbelievers, secularists, and humanists may point to random chance as the most probable answer, religion "ascribes to a divine order that countenances extemporaneous afflictions, natural and personal. God's ways are inscrutable."[7]

Buckley recalled being struck with an overwhelming sense of calm during his 1994 visit. Those who make the trek to Lourdes are able to create their own schedule in conjunction with the administrative offices there, and his began with Mass at the Upper Basilica, one of, as you might imagine, innumerable churches throughout the area.

"I can't offhand remember when last, other than at sea, I felt so little concern for timetables."[7]

His Fridays at Lourdes were filled with what was called the Morning of Recollection, a sacred pause in his infamously busy life. In the serene atmosphere, with time to meditate and reflect, Buckley simply embraced the tranquility of spiritual retreat. Surrounded by the solemnity of the occasion, he was reminded of life's deeper meanings, a perfect complement to the timeless, ethereal feeling Lourdes seemed to evoke. There was also Anointing of the Sick which took place at St. Joseph's Chapel.

There were also strong reminders of our mortality, Buckley noted, of *memento mori,* which tend to be mind-clearing and perspective-enhancing.

Buckley pointed out there were three volunteer-fueled hospices, and while few of his group were ailing, they were nonetheless "reminded that from the day of birth, we are on our deathbeds."

He explained how, while there were thousands of gurneys set aside for *malades* (the catch-all term for sick in France), God-gifted cures are at once not "reasonably expected" and at the same time largely irrelevant as broader perspectives captivate one's mind and attention.

"It is a part of the common faith that prayer can affect anything," Buckley wrote.[7]

Buckley recalled the—in my view—rather extraordinary discovery that the vast majority of those who visit Lourdes are healthy.

While he made the obvious concession that the sick and dying who travel to Lourdes do so because of "the undeniability of recorded miracles," that isn't quite the magnet that captivates, charms, and pulls over 50,000 people to the venerated town every day.[7]

"The reason so many people come, many of them on their second or tenth visit, is that what is effected is a sense of reconciliation, if not well-being."[7]

He joyfully felt a profound sense of "buoyancy" in viewing the great processions and sharing, along with tens of thousands, an underground Mass or the "ambient serenity" he felt for three extraordinary seconds upon being lowered into one of the baths.

"These are Christians feeling impulses of their faith, and intimations of the lady in white," he explained.[7]

Buckley revealed the Catholic contingent is in Lourdes because of "this palpability of the emanations that gave birth to the shrine. The spiritual tonic is felt."[7]

But the parting passages reveal God's love not in dogmatic ritual, but in deed. Buckley recalled, meeting three of the aforementioned *malades* at the Parisian lounge waiting for the airplane. The young man was unable to move without heavy use of a cane.

"He was treated, by this company returning from Lourdes, as a member of the family; which he was, as Lourdes manages to make plain."[7]

It seems worthwhile and in fact unavoidable for anyone with genuine interest in archaeological excursions into Buckley's faith that there was a crucial area where he seemed to divert from the larger Catholic contingent. As with most things, Buckley maintained a somewhat idiosyncratic and nuanced view.

Here, it was actually courtesy of his nephew Friar Michael Bozell, the Benedictine monk of St. Peter's Abbey, also in France, who became a priest.

It was he who gifted his uncle with a few of the hotly contested and controversial writings of the Italian mystic Maria Valtorta.

She infamously penned a gripping and searing tome, five volumes' worth, called *The Poem of Man*.

Part of the fifth volume, by far the most eyebrow-raising, recalled Valtorta's supposedly eyewitness account of Christ's crucifixion.

As one might imagine, her account stirred up terrific fervor within the Vatican as she insisted these writings were a play-by-play of Christ's Passion, a conclusion she came to by way of private vision.

The book spent seventeen years on the Index Librorum Prohibitorum (Index of Prohibited Books). This was the Holy See's list of publications the Catholic Church deemed dangerous or harmful to the faith and morals of Catholics.

The pages that arrived at Buckley's doorstep were accompanied by a note from his nephew.

"The subject of mystical vision is always a touchy matter," it read.[7]

"Sometimes you're dealing with pathological problems rather than supernatural manifestations, and it is almost impossible to make a definitive judgment. That judgment will inevitably hinge on two things: the saintliness of the visionary's life and the integrity of the doctrine implicitly or explicitly contained in the vision."[7]

"It takes awhile for a consensus to materialize. In the meantime, the fate of this or that work can fluctuate."

Buckley's unironic leaning on Valtorta for insight into Christ startled his good friend and noted theological scholar Fr. Michael Fitzpatrick.

Fr. Michael Fitzpatrick expressed concern to William F. Buckley about using private revelations not approved by the church. His unease stemmed not from legalistic objections but from his experience with individuals who seemed unsatisfied with the completeness of divine revelation which ended with the death of the last apostle. He observed how some people approached such writings with an almost insatiable appetite for details about the lives of Christ and the Virgin Mary—details they felt were lacking in the Gospels.

Fitzpatrick explained that these individuals often misunderstood the purpose of the Gospels, which were not intended to serve as biographies of Christ but as proclamations of the Good News of salvation. He emphasized that sacred Scripture contains everything humanity will ever know about the lives of Christ and His mother. For those yearning for more detailed biographies, there was no remedy, though such material could occasionally serve as a tool for private prayer and meditation, provided it was approached with maturity and prudence.

Buckley also drew a comparison between Maria Valtorta's writings and the visions of the 19th-century German nun Anne Catherine Emmerich, whose *The Life of Jesus Christ* shared a similar nature. While Buckley's nephew dismissed Emmerich's accounts as "psychedelic," he found Valtorta's writings evocative of a James Michener novel, blending imaginative narrative with vivid detail.[7]

Buckley, here, made the thoughtful conclusion that the variations of the accounts validate rather than refute the experiences. If they had all been entirely identical, that would raise the most suspicion as to their authenticity.

But that portion of Valtorta's fifth volume had such salience and significance for Buckley it was reprinted, in its entirety, in the "only book on faith" he would ever write as well as in, by the way, his other autobiography, *Miles Gone By: a Literary Autobiography.* There he dedicated an entire chapter so as not to "deprive the reader" of what he viewed as a "great historical event that preceded, and led to, the resurrection, a depiction if not inspired by God, inspiring nonetheless."

This deep reverence for faith was indeed rooted in Buckley's upbringing, but in many ways particularly in the profound influence of his mother, Eloise Steiner Buckley.

He dedicated *Nearer, My God: An Autobiography of Faith* to her, after all, and wrote, "Her worship of Him was as intense as that of the saint transfixed."[7]

He affectionately mused, "Perhaps somewhere else one woman has walked through so many years charming so many people by her warmth and diffidence and humor and faith. If so, I wish I might have known her."

He recalled her beginnings in the South, writing how it was in South Carolina when she was "wonderfully content, making others happy by her vivacity, her delicate beauty, her habit of seeing the best in everyone, the humorous spark in her eye. She never lost a Southern innocence."[7]

As a familial aside, she had a care for language that was undoubtedly passed down, at least in part, to her son.

Buckley noted his oil tycoon father remarked that in forty years of marriage, she never placed a masculine article in front of a masculine noun except on one occasion where she stopped and corrected herself.

Buckley recalled a particularly salient instance of how his mother's "anxiety to do the will of God was more than ritual."[7]

He had once written to his dear mother in early 1963 asking her how she endeavored to reconcile "Christian fraternity with the separation of the races." To put perhaps too fine a point on it, bear in mind that this was at a time and place in the world that was still unforgivably ravaged by the evils of Jim Crow.

"My darling Bill," she answered in her response.

"This is not an answer to your letter, for I cannot answer it too quickly. It came this morning, and, of course, I went as soon as possible to the Blessed Sacrament in our quiet beautiful little church here," she expressed.[7]

"Dear Bill," she went on, "I prayed *so* hard for humility and for wisdom and for guidance from the Holy Spirit. I know He will help me to answer your questions as He thinks they should be answered. I must pray longer before I do this."[7]

Thoughtful consideration in any domain of inquiry should be encouraged, particularly where discussion of God and beliefs are concerned.

His mother was of the most venerated and remarked upon variety of mother, that of the doting kind. She imprinted upon her ten children, Bill of course among them, the admonishment to always respond to a call via the intercoms at the ready in their Connecticut house.

If a child missed their intercom check-in regardless of the time of night, she would "wait up and demand an explanation."[7]

While her vigilant and clear love for her children and their safety was readily on display, it also revealed the depth of her affection and explained the unique lens through which Buckley viewed maternal care.

The anecdote is significant because Buckley wrote that he doubted if his dear mother would have noticed, "half-asleep, if the person on the other end of the line had been God himself, her most reliable friend, and lover."[7]

A second anecdote which rather beautifully cements the relationship between Buckley's mother and him might be when one considered Eloise's grief in the aftermath of the death of her son John which itself was only three months before her own.

WFB said the mourning that sat on his mom's heart was "by her standards, convulsive; but she did not break her rule—she never broke it—which was never, ever to complain; because, she explained, she could never repay God the favors He had done her, no matter what tribulations she might be made to suffer."

A bout with pneumonia would remand the matriarch of the Buckley family to a hospital in Sharon, Connecticut.

Five days before her death in April 1985, she went an entire week without uttering so much as a syllable.

The nurse would bring her from the bathroom over to her armchair and would, quite lovingly, adorn the eighty-nine-year-old with makeup, lipstick, and pearls.

Upon seeing her face in a mirror, she turned to her nurse and, with a wry smile, said, "Isn't it amazing that anyone so old can be so beautiful?"[7]

"God's creature," Buckley penned, no doubt with adoration in his heart and perhaps a tear in his eye. "Well done, Lord. My Lord. Our Lord."[7]

Father Gerald Murray, a canon lawyer and the pastor of New York City's Holy Family Church, who was a chaplain on that trip to Lourdes, wrote, "Bill Buckley was a pilgrim who sought and upheld truth and goodness in the great struggle against the 20th-century's promoters of lies and evil. We are all in his debt."[8]

Yet another man of the cloth, Father Joseph A. Marcello, who helped research *Nearer, My God* reflected, "When I met Mr. Buckley, I was a sophomore in college, and even at a distance of all these years, I know that what most struck me about him then was what might be called a certain Catholic matter-of-factness: not in the sense of nonchalance in approaching matters of faith, but just the opposite. From his lifetime of familiarity with the Lord came an ease of conversation about Him and a givenness that his life was firmly situated within the context of a lived discipleship in the middle of the Church."[8]

In *National Review*, conservative social commentator Roger Kimball wrote, "Everyone knows that Bill commanded a formidable vocabulary. It was significant, therefore, that he should have telephoned us once in search of a word. 'It means taking pleasure in the misfortune of others,' he said to my wife. 'Schadenfreude?' she ventured. 'That's it!' he said and rang off. How perfectly Buckleyesque that he should have forgotten it. It named an emotion that was as foreign to him as joy was native."[8]

Following Buckley's passing, *National Review* published an article[8] recounting the experiences of various people who had met him. Each story was nearly identical: Buckley treated them as if they were the most important person in the world. Priests and at least one religious sister shared how his public Catholicism influenced them. This experience was evident in his interactions with both friends and, perhaps with doubled and tripled effect, his adversaries.

In today's polarized political climate, Buckley's life can serve as evidence, one arrived at via his piety, of the value of civil discourse.

His ability to enjoy the ethereal sweetness of friendships across ideological divides was far from a signal of ideological weakness or compromise but a testament to his strength of character and the depth of his—to invoke a fashionable term with my apologies—tolerance.

He demonstrated, simply by living out the Christian ethic of love, it is possible to hold firm beliefs while still respecting and valuing those who see the world differently.

Buckley's life was a testament to the power of faith and, to resort to the wisdom of countless after-school specials, friendship.

His Catholicism provided him with a moral North Star guiding him in all his interactions and allowing him to forge bonds with individuals across the political spectrum. In doing so, he not only enriched his own life but also contributed to a more thoughtful and compassionate public discourse.

His commitment to his faith and the guiding principles springing from it serve to demonstrate how faith and friendship can coexist, even—and perhaps especially—in the face of profound disagreement.

"Sin," Buckley noted, "is largely ignored in progressive circles where divine sanctions are simply immaterial; and this is an important social development."[7]

"Whatever became of sin?" Buckley inquired.

He may as well have postulated the question last week.

Yet this question underscores a far more pressing crisis: a loss of national purpose. The very fabric of society, once woven together by shared values, has begun to come apart. Where once there was a moral compass to guide public and private life, we now see the horrifying effects of moral relativism and subjective "truths" run amok.

The decline in religious and ethical foundations, as Buckley foretold, is not merely a spiritual crisis but a reflection of a deeper, more existential void. Without a cohesive moral or cultural framework, the nation risks losing sight of its collective goals and identity, drifting aimlessly on a sea of ephemeral ideologies with no what we might deem bedrock orientation, with only superficial pursuits.

We have lost that sense of purpose in many ways in the United States. A possible—dare I say probable?—explanation would be the "progressively" advanced ideal that the West in general and the United States specifically are irreversibly tainted by the sins of white supremacy, institutional racism, supposed patriarchal oppression, and all the rest of the boring liberal tropes that have come to preoccupy cultural discussions and debates.

In a 1968 interview, Buckley identified a deeper restlessness at play, one he traced to the excesses of rationalism and liberalism. He argued how liberalism, by promising happiness could be found through government solutions, led people to rely on what he called "narcotic substitutes"—temporary distractions provided by government agencies—rather than seeking happiness and contentment in their religion, culture, or institutions or within themselves.[10]

In a private, previously unseen April 1971 letter direct from Buckley in the then-*National Review* offices at 150 East 35th Street to a charitable donor in South Carolina, Buckley intimated even then that along with "economic uncertainty," Americans were being burdened with a "philosophical uncertainty," which he characterized as simply "the great doubt held by so many about the future of America".[11]

Buckley believed this shift undermined America's spiritual foundation, which he saw as critical to its greatness. As he put it, "This is why America ceases to be as idealistically magnetic as it has been in the past."[10] For Buckley, only by returning to those traditional sources of meaning, especially religion, could America regain its sense of purpose and avoid the moral and spiritual decline brought on by excessive dependence on government.

This book is by no means meant to be a polemic or attack against the Left as such. To the contrary, it is a general admonishment to all sides of the political spectrum and a call to return to civility in our day.

Nonetheless, it has to be noticed these points have unquestionably shaped much of the discourse coming from the Left largely because it has been the primary force infiltrating and controlling institutions like academia and journalism, to name just a few.

That reality is not my fault, and it is information of which I am a prisoner. I can't *not* notice it. Rest assured, if it were the Right which had captured these institutions, I would be just as critical, for to do so would be a Buckleyinian job given his animus toward the fanatical fringes pervading his side.

This sort of anti-intellectual plague, a downstream effect of hypertribalism, has attacked all traditional institutions, not the least of which is Buckley's beloved church.

Churches—because they are not God's efforts to reach down to us in the material, temporal world, but rather are our man-made and therefore inherently fallible effort to reach up to God—have very much become waterlogged from this downstream effect.

It was in early 2021 when the Episcopal Church published a self-flagellating "racial audit."[12] One can almost sense what the audit will say before opening the cover.

That audit, by the way, cost the church over $1 million. One suspects there were more deserving efforts the church might have chosen that could have used a cash infusion. (A whole other book, by the way, lurks beneath the opportunity losses of this kind in our day.)

But the audit covered 2018 through to 2020 and found the church guilty of the charge of racism to quite literally no one's shock.

With a few more-than-questionable presuppositions already baked into its thesis, the audit's goal was not "to determine whether or not systemic racism exists in the Episcopal Church, but rather to examine its effects and the dynamics by which it is maintained in the Church structure. It was critical to approach this objective with openness, rather than starting with pre-existing assumptions and conclusions. To this end, we have employed the guiding tools of grounded theory and the theoretical framework of critical race theory."[12]

One immediately steps into semantic and conversational quicksand here, but the Church did slightly redefine, may I say rechristen, CRT to mean "a social and theoretical framework that understands race as a lens through which to seek understanding of the world. It insists, like critical theory at large, that social problems are created by structures and institutions, rather than by individuals. Numerous scholars have contributed to the work of critical race theory, including Derrick Bell, Kimberle Williams Crenshaw, Richard Delgado, and others."[12]

It is, indeed, a predictable instance of white guilt coupled with performative virtue signaling (what other kind is there?). After all, Episcopal Bishop of New York Andrew Dietsche made the progressive move of listing Ibram X. Kendi's *How to Be an Antiracist* as its diocesan book study.

Far from an urging against tribalism and its toxic effects, as Buckley would have, this is a direct warrant for and incitement to that tribalism.

As a proper serf to the progressive cause, Bishop Dietsche promised Kendi's gaslighting tome (my words of course, not his) would get to the moral bedrock of "the deep currents of racism in our society and institutions."[13]

The bishop sang a predictable song in 2020 when he, somewhat ominously pontificated that "a time of reckoning has come for a country and its systems rooted in white supremacy."[13]

Douglas Murray focuses on this explicitly in his *War On the West*. He reveals the bishop said, of course with no real authority or evidence, "unacknowledged racist assumptions infect every institution and system and my heart and mind, and yours too."[13] This is the Kendi-flavored gaslighting I am referring to. How could this bishop—who doesn't know me, likely doesn't know you, and, by the way, whom I never wish to meet—possibly know the ravages of my own mind? Is there not a fallacious element lurking there as well?

When the bishop should have been extolling the virtues of a different book more central to his faith, he instead stated with a dialectic dash of self-righteousness and self-piety, that "reading this book convicted me, but made me grateful."[13]

So this was the sort of observation of nonbias the Church brought to its race audit.

Murray coined a new phrase which I wouldn't mind seeing accelerated in our culture: *Kendi-ism*.

In the report, it did indeed seem if the bishop was anxious to anoint anyone, it wasn't Christ; it was Kendi.

But almost 80 percent of the Episcopal Church leadership (77 percent, to be precise) defined *racism* not as believing the human species is subdivided by races, which would be my own. Nor did they define it as the intention to harm or actual harm of another group based on the immutable characteristic of their race.

But racism was "a combination of racial prejudice or discrimination, a system that grants power to one social group."[12]

In the depressingly post-definition world in which we live, the salient point here—the only one really worth retaining—is, racism was defined as a system of power and thus far harder to see, let alone ameliorate, without simply tearing the entire system asunder and starting anew.

One suspects quite quickly that was the goal all along.

But the study is a master class in creating a mystery where none exists.

The study, far from objectively condemning the church on charges of racism, seems to swing in the opposite direction.

Both the white leadership and the BIPOC (Black, Indigenous, and People of Color) leadership (there's something putrescent about separating human beings in that way, but we'll put that aside for now) reported near-identical levels of "respect" with regard to how they felt they were being treated.[13]

The study—in a move I will let you, dear reader, decide whether is racist or not—endeavored to identify respondents in the study purely by their race. By my lights, that is the same tactic the revolting David Duke would employ were he to become a statistician.

So, the study, identifying the person only as a "white, churchwide leader," attributed to that "white" him or her or, at this point, they the statement "The Episcopal Church has to stop being so white."[12]

Someone else, this time listed as a "person of color, churchwide leader" said, "There's war. We're in the middle of a war, and I don't know why people don't seem to be behaving as if we should be . . . We're gearing up for a fight for our very existence, Black people in this country. We have a Black head of the Church, but the institution is institutionalized."[12]

I hope this particular example does not strike you, dear reader, as parochial with regard to our culture in general. One point to glean from this is the gaslighting and utterly unwinnable nature of this particular mode of "discussion." Murray brought this to bear when he noted a great barrier crops up when combating the supposed systemic racism of the church in having to negotiate the minefield of defensiveness when it is "named as a problem."[13]

That other great patron saint of antiracism intrudes here. Robin D'Angelo, as Murray puts it, would prescribe "the best way for the church to be not racist is for it to be unbothered when it is accused of institutional racism."[13]

The audit further advocates, predictably, for the "multifaceted approach" of "reparation and redistribution of wealth." But because nothing is ever straightforward with this line of thinking, this redistribution should be attempted without "exacerbating the problems of racism and white dominant culture." So there is evidently a racist way of approaching the nonracist ideal.

This insipid ethic has also intruded into Buckley's beloved Holy See.

It was in the summer of 2020 when Reverend Daniel Patrick Moloney, the Catholic chaplain of the Massachusetts Institute of Technology, sent a fierce and bravely worded email to the college's Catholic community saying George Floyd had "not lived a virtuous life" and committed the most egregious sin of all when he wrote, "Most people in the country have framed this as an act of racism. I don't think we know that." He doubled down in the same email when he wrote that we simply cannot know if racism dwells at the heart of the American police as they have to "deal with dangerous and bad people all the time, and that often hardens them."

Well, the email left a devastating path riddled with outrage in its wake.

All the usual suspects came out to talk about how victimized they felt by the email.

The vice president and dean for student life responded publicly that Father Moloney's email was "deeply disturbing." While noting how the good reverend was "devaluing and disparaging" of George Floyd's character, the official took a page right out of Kendi by saying Father Moloney failed to acknowledge "systemic racism." Buckley would cringe at this commitment to proceeding on false premises.

Father Moloney was, of course, asked to apologize by the powers that be, and because apologies never satisfy a mob, he was asked to resign.

But the aftereffects of an institution like the Catholic Church convicting themselves of racism, both historically and at the present moment, is that people will believe them. This has, Buckley would likely have pointed out, torn apart the previously quite sturdy social fabric that organizations like the church provide.

Murray points out, soberingly, that when this is how the great religious institutions of our day view themselves and—in a turn both masochistic and sadistic in its way—advertise this rather stridently, people unfamiliar with the church's history or influence will take them at their word.

Faith, as Buckley understood it, was not an abstract exercise in self-flagellation or conformity to passing ideological trends. Rather, it was a profound orientation toward truth, humility, and the ultimate good, a guardrail against the corrosive forces of tribalism and the nihilism forming from it. The failures of religious institutions to uphold these ideals are not only symptomatic of larger societal decay but also a warning to all who seek a moral compass.

It is in this context that Buckley's commitment to decency becomes inseparable from his faith. His belief in civility, respect, and intellectual rigor—values shared even with ideological adversaries like John Kenneth Galbraith—emerges as a natural outgrowth of his spiritual convictions. If faith offered the foundation, decency was the structure he built upon it, providing a model for navigating our polarized era with grace and principle.

CHAPTER 2

Friendship Across the Aisle: William F. Buckley Jr.'s Legacy of Unity

Ralph Waldo Emerson famously wrote, "A friend may well be reckoned the masterpiece of nature."

William F. Buckley Jr. seemed to understand this above all else. It might seem odd that a particularly opinionated polemicist such as Buckley would be capable of friendships with those he disagreed with, let alone for him to prefer their company, but that often seemed to be the case.

It was, of course, *National Review* that served as Buckley's platform for the promulgation and proliferation of the new conservative agenda. It would be *National Review* as well as *Firing Line* that would become Buckley's most enduring legacies. *National Review* would also, even at its founding, demonstrate Buckley's perhaps surprising ability to unify those around him.

It was at the urging of an Austrian journalist named Willi Schlamm that Buckley would create the vaunted conservative journal.

Schlamm came from *The Freeman*, itself a conservative journal of opinion that found itself drifting further and further toward covering economic issues and, by definition, diminishing its relevance in the greater cultural war.

Alas, Schlamm held ideological eccentricities even Buckley couldn't reconcile. He lasted two years at *NR*, a time Priscilla Buckley called, simply, "tumultuous." According to Bill's sister, who was also the managing editor, Schlamm thought he could influence, perhaps even manipulate, the then-twenty-nine-year-old Buckley and circumvent him to run the offices of *National Review*. Buckley, unsurprisingly, would turn out to be a hard person to outsmart, and after a number of outbursts, off into the wilderness Schlamm went.

Still, Buckley did not build *National Review* alone. He was joined by a diverse group of intellectuals, each bringing their own distinct ideological slant to the publication. James Burnham, a former Marxist turned staunch anticommunist, contributed his analytical rigor to the editorial team. Willmoore Kendall, one of Buckley's Yale professors, lent his fiery populist spirit, while Priscilla Buckley, his sister, managed the magazine's operations with precision and grace.

The infamously nocturnal Frank Meyer helped shape the fusionist philosophy blending libertarian and traditionalist elements, and L. Brent Bozell Jr., Buckley's brother-in-law (and later ghostwriter of the hugely influential right-wing tome *The Conscience of a Conservative*, nominally penned by Barry Goldwater) offered his sharp legal mind and strong Catholic convictions. William Rusher, a key figure in conservative political strategy, provided the magazine with his enviable talents as publisher.

Together, these founding editors formed an unlikely coalition, unified under Buckley's leadership to advance an ideologically coherent and politically potent conservative movement.

In an illuminating *New Yorker* article, published in 2005 courtesy of Tom Reiss spoke of the *Up from Liberalism* author's effect on the conservative movement, cheerfully designating Buckley a "reconciler."

"Buckley, despite his rhetoric, was a reconciler, and an institution builder; his goal was to see conservatism become a politically dominant mass movement. To that end, in an effort to unite libertarians, traditionalists, and anticommunists, Buckley endeavored to create *National Review*.

Reiss adds that Buckley was able to accomplish the daunting task of "encouraging contributors to attack liberals when they might have preferred to attack each other."

Bill Rusher, the man who would be for thirty years the publisher of *National Review*, expounded on this

> Who, or what, could bring the prickly components of the conservative movement together and induce it to speak with a single journalistic voice?

Who could proclaim and refine conservatism's fundamental principles, resolve or compromise disputes on internal issues, promote intellectual and political spokesmen, and lead the philosophical battle against both communism and modern liberalism? Who, but William F. Buckley?[9]

Priscilla Buckley, who took up the mantle of managing editor for forty-three years, particularly noticed the internal schism between Meyer and Burnham. She sharpened Rusher's point, in print, that the major ideological division between the two as well as the founding group in general would have downed the journalistic excursion were it not for the unifying force which Buckley's character provided.

There was also constant disagreement between Meyer and a conservative icon in his own right, Russell Kirk, the man who, two years prior to the founding of *NR*, penned the political mainstay *The Conservative Mind*. And there was, as Priscilla put it, the issue of Burnham's "political pragmatism" which would endlessly irk Rusher and the third *Bill* of this swashbuckling enterprise, Bill Rickenbacker, son of World War 1 flying ace Eddie Rickenbacker and *NR*'s editorial writer.

But schisms, annoyances, and garden-variety disagreements never escalated into rage-filled conclusions because of Buckley's magnanimous nature and his genius at dealing with intelligent and volatile characters.

So, it was in 1955, *National Review* was founded and served primarily as an anchor for the bolstering and unification of conservative sentiment in America.

Before its founding, it was a popular consensus in public discourse that conservatism in America was rather fractious, disorganized, and lacked a common cause among its supporters. *National Review* served as a bonding agent for this broken movement.

One of the more revolutionary focuses of *National Review* was the promotion of fusionism among its constituents. *Fusionism* is the joining of classically liberal or libertarian viewpoints with traditional Edmund Burke conservatism into a new symbiotic iteration of conservatism.

It was this ethic of fusionism that enabled Buckley and *National Review* to clearly define, for a national audience, what a conservative was and most certainly was not. This may sound simple, but it can be quite hard to get a large audience to agree on a set definition of something, particularly on an ideology, and most particularly on that most charged and sensitive of ideologies: political ideology.

Prime and frequent targets of the editors and writers of *National Review* were the vulgar George Wallace, governor of Alabama, the man who once intimated in an interview with *Time Magazine* that he would never be "out-segged." It was late January 1968, when the wretched Wallace appeared on *Firing Line* to defend his positions against the rapier skill and wit of its host.

Mr. Buckley told the audience in his introduction of Wallace that a refusal to be "out-segged" is to "say that he would not permit his opponent ever again to take a position more pronounced than his own in favor of racial segregation."

Buckley and the *National Review* faithful also raged against the John Birch Society and its founder, Robert Welch. The JBS was a rather unfortunate but nonetheless influential organization best characterized by its far-right or ultraconservative politics.

No crusade during Buckley's half-century on the national political stage did more to solidify his reputation as a gatekeeper of the conservative movement—or consumed more of his time—than his battle against the John Birch Society. Founded by Robert Welch in 1958, as a vehicle to shape public policy, the JBS became a major focus of Buckley's efforts. By 1961, he noted to a supporter of *National Review* and the JBS that discussions about the organization had overshadowed even his debates on the existence of God or the financial challenges facing *National Review*.

It was this platform, along with the formation of *Firing Line*, a political debate show hosted by Buckley on PBS, that catapulted Buckley into the public eye and solidified his status as the premier champion of the new conservative cause.

Among early ideological commitments was the magazine's rather salient advocacy for the politics of

Mr. Goldwater, including the spreading of fiscal conservatism as well as a stout repudiation of communism in America. *National Review*'s fealty to Mr. Goldwater was so strong that the vaunted and established magazine played a pivotal role in the "Draft Goldwater" movement of both his 1960 and 1964 presidential efforts.

There is even a common thread of generosity and a kind of transideological bonding woven through Buckley's hiring process.

The first, second, third, and fourth priorities of the magazine were that its writing would be clean, intelligible, and, above all, distinguished.

Buckley's and Frank Meyer's recruitment strategy was fairly straightforward. It would begin with a simple telephone call which ended with Meyer or Buckley (whoever it may be) asking the would-be writer at the other end of the line to pen what they called a brief. This was a 150- to 250-word book review. If all was well following the filing of the requested review, it was, as Managing Editor Priscilla Buckley put it, "so much to the good." If it was not well, the relationship would seldom last.

Buckley's sister noted, I think rather extraordinarily, "it seemed more important to [Buckley] that a writer write beautiful prose than that the writer be a movement conservative."[25]

Out of that ethic springs the surprising reality that some of *NR*'s early contributors were never conservative. Among them were future noted critic and forever lefty John Leonard, no doubt grateful to Buckley for giving him his first job in journalism.

There were also those who might have started out on the Right but gradually shifted toward the Left end of the Overton window. These would include future Nixon antagonist Gary Wills as well as noted author Joan Didion, who would go on to become, along with Norman

Mailer, a key figure in the New Journalism movement, and her husband, John Dunne, who would see the words tumbling out of his pen spill onto the pages of the hardly Right-leaning *Harper's*, *Vanity Fair*, and *New York Review of Books.*

The common bond these figures had—and the only one Buckley really cared about—was that they were craftsmen (and women) of beautiful prose. That value shows a willingness to overlook political fealty in search of a great common cause.

Here, Buckley may have, if only by deed (which is the most crucial), invoked Romans 14:19, "Let us therefore make every effort to do what leads to peace and to mutual edification." [Bible 2]

There is a lesson for modern society lurking beneath that, isn't there?

But friends should be like books in a well-curated library: carefully chosen for their wisdom and depth.

Buckley was by no means at all flagrant or careless with whom he chose to associate or be friends. Of course, anybody of ordinary morality would, regardless of how generous and personally amicable they might be, nonetheless have their moral last ditch. That is when the extent of one's political fealty becomes so indefensible the Venn diagram of politics and morality becomes an almost perfect circle.

For Buckley, to his credit, it was Nazism and antisemitism that were the trip wires of his last ditch. He famously fired writer Joseph Sobran from *National Review* for what he deemed to be "contextually antisemitic" prose. This was on the question of Israel. Politics truly is nothing if not redundant.

He would also voluntarily and quickly disengage from a friendship he had with Revilo Oliver after the latter made stalwart and unforgivable moves to the fringes of fanatical conservatism that typically held sway for Nazis (he advised holocaust denial groups) and antisemitism (he would go on to cofound the dreaded John Birch Society). No small thing considering Oliver was on the masthead of *National Review* and Buckley once called him, "without exception, the most erudite man I've ever known."

But one of the central and unmistakable markers of Buckley's almost universal magnanimity would be his friendship with the troubled but unquestionably brilliant Norman Mailer. The two men held diametrically opposed views, and Mailer's famously thuggish and confrontational nature lent an air of impossibility to the idea of them being friends.

Buckley's capacity for friendship goes far beyond Mr. Mailer. His feeling for *transideological bonding*, to coin a phrase, had an effect as far as the liberal Pulitzer Prize-winning journalist Murray Kempton, who in his book *Rebellions, Perversities, and Main Events,* inscribed "*For William F. Buckley, Jr., genius at friendships that surpass all understanding.*"

Buckley also would fiercely stand by his friends even when it might not have been considered politically wise to do so. Mr. Buckley publicly lent his support to Allard Lowenstein, the Democratic congressman in New York. *The New York Times* reported that Buckley "endorsed Allard K. Lowenstein, who is not only the Democratic candidate for Congress in the Fifth Congressional District here, but also was long considered the wunderkind of the liberal, antiwar wing of the Democratic Party."

Mr. Buckley, the columnist, hailed Mr. Lowenstein as "among the two or three most able and conscientious Democrats running for national office." That was good for Mr. Lowenstein since he was running in a heavily Republican district."

But more about Kempton, Mailer, Lowenstein, and others—as Buckley would say on his program—in due course.

When Buckley died in 2008, his funeral at St. Patrick's Cathedral in New York was a smattering of overlapping, conflicting, and utterly irreconcilable political sensibilities. Who else but Buckley could compel the infamous atheist Christopher Hitchens to walk into a church and—as Mr. Buckley's son, Christopher, put it—"belt out 'He Who Would Valiant Be'?"

There, the curious observer saw the former Democrat mayor of New York City Ed Koch, friend and statesman Henry Kissinger, and former senator George McGovern, the 1972 Democratic candidate for president. Buckley's funeral, much like his life, captured his genius at friendships. A genius which can, perhaps, serve as a model in our own increasingly tribal and ideologically divided time.

To step into a Rod Serlingesque role, imagine if you will anything like those waves of affection pulsating on the shores of today's divisive climate.

There is hateful rhetoric run amok from both sides of the aisle, making the possibility of friendships of the kind that sweetened Buckley's life out of the question.

The mental poison of tribalism is that most venomous of cultural snakes which must indeed be cut off straight from the head.

On the macro policy-driven level, most will be able to summon in their mind their favorite example of this.

Liberal Congresswoman Alexandra Ocasio-Cortez proudly and unproductively referred to migrant detention centers at the border as "concentration camps." You perhaps, dear reader, could gather from something about my last name the scale of the shiver that ran laps up and down my spine and the rictus of loathing that pounced on my face and fanned out like a galaxy. And I wasn't alone, believe me.

But those on the Right are far from immune to this kind of vituperation.

Staying with border security, my boxing-informed ethic of punching above the belt was similarly offended when the Republican representative from Georgia, Marjorie Taylor Greene, was shown heckling President Biden during his State of the Union speech in early 2024. Greene's behavior was, ostensibly, because she wanted the 81-year-old president to acknowledge the murder of a Georgia nursing student, Laken Riley, by an undocumented worker the previous month.

While there may be a faint shadow of a point here, as with AOC, the vitriol signals something far more than a simple good-faith disagreement. The self-evident toss of the political pigskin along with the unmistakable performance art so common in attention-seeking narcissistic behavior underscores the "discourse" fracturing our cultural climate. This useless slacktivism has so poisonously contributed to the tribalism we see in today's society.

Buckley would be repulsed.

Rich Lowry also stalwartly addressed Buckley's views on tribalism: "He would be against tribalism insofar as its anti-thought, anti-persuasion, and anti-reason. You just sign up for a group and stick with them without independent thought. Buckley was individualistic through and through and valued independent thought. He wouldn't like the idea of subordinating what he believed to any tribe, nor would he like anyone else doing the same."

Lowry added, "Despite Buckley's individualism, he was fiercely defensive of his views and conservatism. He could depart from the tribe when necessary," noting the Panama Canal episode on *Firing Line*. As he sat opposite his great friend and *National Review* subscriber Ronald

Reagan, Buckley gave us a famous example of his willingness to go his own way:

> Buckley probably would hate how much we just line up and take one source of information that confirms what we already think and then present that as our views. That's not the way he operated or thought American politics and society should ideally operate.

Journalist Hendrik Hertzberg seems to agree, opining how Buckley "could not have been happy with the vulgarity of the movement he did so much to spawn."

Say what you wish about Buckley's views toward McCarthyism or his only slightly less than full-throated support of Francisco Franco's regime in Spain, Buckley's "genius at friendship" and Catholic ethic of tolerance and love would have rendered today's behavior utterly unthinkable to him, to put it mildly.

The tribal vitriol dividing America today has deep roots and complex causes, reaching beyond mere ideological differences. Political discourse has become a battleground where respect and humility are casualties, replaced by an unyielding cycle of resentment and suspicion. This book seeks to explore how we arrived at this polarized state and, more important, to consider the ways we might find our way back to a more respectful, compassionate ethos.

In the following pages, like the green light beckoning to Gatsby, we'll look to William F. Buckley Jr.'s life as a beacon of civility in an age where that shine of civility has all but dimmed. Buckley's friendships with ideological adversaries, his advocacy for intellectual curiosity, and his deep-seated sense of gratitude offer antidotes to the fanaticism and schism currently gripping our society.

Central to Buckley's beliefs was his faith, a guiding force informing his actions and shaping his worldview. He would argue with conviction that a renewed orientation toward God is essential to transcending today's hypertribalism and to rooting our national character in something deeper than ideology.

We already covered that which meant the most to Buckley—his faith—as the key principle he embodied to counteract societal divides, while later sections will expand on values such as decency, honesty in journalism, honesty in academia, the pursuit of truth, the rejection of fanaticism, humor, and forgiveness. Each principle builds upon the last, laying out a blueprint for how we might resist today's pervasive tribalism, strengthen our institutions, and foster genuine dialogue.

Ultimately, Buckley's legacy and his faith suggest that even in a polarized era, a return to these principles can help us restore the balance we've lost and guide us toward a more unified, spiritually grounded national character.

CHAPTER 3

Norman Mailer: A Friendship of Opposites

The saga of the curious friendship between Buckley and the famed author Norman Mailer was in many ways stranger than fiction. They were ideological mirrors of each other. But both ran unsuccessful campaigns for mayor; in fact, both ran unsuccessful campaigns for mayor of the same city, New York. Both started quite influential political publications.

In Mailer's case, it was *The Village Voice*, and of course *National Review* in Buckley's. They were best-selling authors when they were quite young. Finally, and most surprisingly in many ways, they were opponents of the Liberal Establishment. The similarities don't stop there. They also went to Ivy League schools and were World War II veterans. This is quite fertile ground for a friendship to blossom. It was, of course, daily complicated by their diametrically opposed political views.

After all, if Vietnam could divide a country, think what it might do to a friendship, as Mailer and Buckley strongly disagreed on American intervention in Vietnam, though it didn't intrude greatly. Friendship is indeed possible within the brackets of political disagreement. It is particularly noteworthy, however, in Mailer's case that he should have been amenable to a social relationship, let alone friendly social relations with Buckley. After all, Mailer earned a well-deserved reputation for intellectual thuggishness compounded by a number of public feuds. One may recall a rather infamous appearance Mailer made on *The Dick Cavett Show* on December 1, 1971.

He appeared on the talk show along with journalist Janet Flanner and the one and only Gore Vidal. Mailer, who seemed fairly drunk, refused to shake Vidal's hand after being introduced and briskly took to insulting both guests and the host. As an aside, Mrs. Flanner emerges as the unlikely star of the affair as she looks directly at a drunk and bloviating Mailer, tells him she is "becoming very, very bored," and subsequently blows him a kiss. Of course, one could reasonably argue that Buckley's and Mailer's shared animus of Vidal would be a bonding agent for the two of them.

Many do seem to miss those various bonding agents in the chemical makeup of the Buckley-Mailer friendship. In addition to their similarities and their shared repudiation of the Liberal Establishment, the two men had a shared hatred of what Kevin Schultz in his book *Buckley and Mailer: The Difficult Friendship That Shaped the Sixties* defined as the "deadening technological bureaucratization in a grand scheme to create something more fulfilling, more in touch with what it means to be human."

It was their concurrent ascension to the oft-repeated although admittedly vague titles of *public intellectuals* that was the great engine behind the two men.

They first met in the fall of 1962. Buckley wrote in his 2007 obituary for his friend that "Mailer's career intersected with my own when in September 1962 two entrepreneurs rented the Medinah Temple in Chicago, which held over 4,000 people, and engaged Mailer and me to debate on the nature of the right wing in American politics. It pleased Mailer, who was complaining widely about his poverty, that *Playboy* magazine immediately contracted to publish his and my opening statements in its next issue."

Mailer certainly held Buckley in high esteem. He once wrote to a friend that Buckley was "the leading young Conservative in the country, and in fact, the most important Conservative in the public eye after Barry Goldwater."

So it came to pass that an ambitious and passionate promoter by the name of Robert Golden made the plans to bring the two together to debate. For their parts, Mailer and Buckley quickly accepted Golden's invitation to battle out their ideas before an educated and literate audience. In a piece of shrewd dealing, Golden rather wisely set the debate in the same city and only two days apart from the heavyweight championship match between Sonny Liston and Floyd Patterson.

It is suggested Golden was likely aiming to construct a stark dichotomy between good and evil. One might wonder where, on this spectrum, Golden believed evil should fall. There is considerable evidence to support the idea Golden would have placed it on the side of Norman Mailer. After all, Golden's promotional material for the event described Buckley as "the forceful philosopher of The New Conservatism . . ." and positioned him against "America's angry young man and Leading Radical." Typically, labeling someone as "angry" suggests a characterization focusing on emotional intensity, leaving little room for nuanced ideological discussion.

So, on September 22, 1962, in front of a sold-out crowd, the two men went back and forth with the purpose of the debate and rather general resolution "What Is the Real Nature of the Right Wing in America?" The two agreed on fairly surprising points, most saliently a disgust with what had come to be known as the Liberal Establishment.

They also had a tête-à-tête regarding such varied subjects as religion and communism (which Buckley detested in almost fanatical style). They would go on to duke it out over civil rights, state's rates, and politics in general. The debate was certainly illuminating for the audience. Incidentally, in the audience, one would have found a wide-eyed twenty-five-year-old college graduate by the name of Abbie Hoffman who would, of course, go on to be one of the most vocal and prominent antiwar activists of the sixties.

The curious observation needing to be made is, the two men were "near allies in the battle to overturn the Liberal Establishment."

This is so surprising upon the quiet realization that Mailer was a radical and Buckley was, of course, a right-winger.

In Buckley's opening statement of that debate, he turned a vengeful eye toward the Liberal Establishment and fumed, "The Liberal community accept[ed] calmly and fatalistically the march of events of the past years." This was a slam against the liberals for their not-at-all meager work toward the proliferation of communism in Russia as well as in the Eastern Bloc of Europe and China, and Buckley offered the usual conservative gripes of the various avenues of government overreach, including increasing taxes and excess regulation.

But that was only on the level of policy. On the moral level, from which in many ways springs political fealty, Buckley said the liberal community had no moral "ground wire," readily surrendering "an operative set of values" when it became convenient to do so:

> For [liberals], there is no ground wire, and without the grounding, the voltage fluctuates wildly, wantonly, chasing after the immediate line of least resistance.

When it was his turn, Mailer surprised everyone and perhaps himself by finding he agreed with a central thesis of Buckley's argument: a shared revulsion of the Establishment liberals.

The Armies of the Night: History as a Novel, the Novel as History author (which wouldn't be published for six more years), Mailer went on his own rampage about the Left's inability to provide solutions to the various social and cultural landmines set off in the aftermath of World War II. He called it, in what was surely an ever-intensifying agreement with Buckley, that it was liberals and of course liberalism that was the curtain-raiser to the ill-advised Cold War which was powered by a faux-commitment to Christianity.

Mailer went on to rant the Left that had manufactured "a deterioration in desire, an apathy about the future, a detestation of the present, an amnesia of the past. Its forms are many, its flavor is unforgettable: it is a disease which destroys flavor."

When two sides agree on everything, that becomes a very serious problem in a debate. Mailer's antidote was to say Buckley and his conservatives were no better, saying half the so-called conservatives were, in fact, conservative in name only, to call upon a familiar political slur. He further accused those on the Right, Buckley among them, of caring primarily for preserving the business class as well as Red-baiting about communism. He said in truth, this was simply a kind of moral smokescreen and at its core, it was laissez-faire capitalism that was the great calling for the Right.

So, one heard Mailer's concessions and his provocations in one fell swoop.

As to who won the debate, that really would depend on whom you asked.

But while a debate might seem to be an odd way of initiating a friendship, perhaps it isn't quite so odd considering the happy warriors under examination. They seemed able to separate, as it were, the debate from the debater.

Here Buckley—and Mailer, though he would blush at the accusation of living out a Christian value in any way—lived the worth-repeating passage Colossians 3:12–14, "Therefore, as God's chosen people, holy and dearly loved, clothe yourselves with compassion, kindness, humility, gentleness and patience. Bear with each other and forgive one another. . . And over all these virtues put on love, which binds them all together in perfect unity." [Bible - 6]

A few months after the debate, Mailer gave a speech at the University of Chicago. There was a Q & A and, sure enough, he was asked his opinion on Buckley. While he had no problem categorizing Buckley's style of debate as "unspeakably churlish invective," he did warmly relent that the radical Catholic right-winger was "the best fellow you ever met off stage."

Gay Talese published in a column on September 24 for *The New York Times* how he believed it to be a draw. His headline simply read "Mailer Debates William Buckley: Chicago Political Bout a Draw."

But their friendship had indeed been a difficult one. Buckley called Mailer a "moral pervert" in a *National*

Review column now preserved in infamy called "Listen, Mills" in December 1960.

Standing in contrast with the ideal American conservative, Buckley wrote, there are "clusters of truths which are loosely referred to as our 'Judeo-Christian tradition' [as]—well . . . truths."

In that 1962 invective, Buckley asserted that Mailer and men like him "chase about wildly through hipsterism and existentialism and humanism and Freudianism and communism and fascism and objectivism and what have you. Just to say you've got the blackboard clean."

Toward the end of the allotted column space, Buckley did at least give half a shot at a compliment by noting "even if he doesn't know what it is that he wants to say, [Mailer's] desperate anxiety to say it, fired by his incandescent moral energy, makes him very much worth watching."

Mailer, for his part, had some kind words in defense of Buckley to deploy as well.

When asked about the *National Review* founder in the weeks after the debate, Mailer noted, "Buckley's all right, a charming guy, a dirty fighter, and fun to debate with." Even that minimum of recognizing a debate as fun is a cultural status quo I wouldn't mind returning to. Nowadays terms like *debate, argument,* etc. are almost exclusively referred to in the pejorative sense.

In *Buckley and Mailer* Kevin Schultz pointed out how both men were calling on America and, of course, Americans to "live up to its better angels." Not coincidentally, that is exactly what I am calling for with the publication of the words you're reading now. But for Mailer and Buckley, the problem was, they disagreed on what those angels might say.

Yet one can discern a clear, if slightly tenuous, affection among the provocations.

But the success of the debate, aided in no small way by its publication in *Playboy*—which made that particular issue the highest-selling of the time—encouraged Mailer to seek out Buckley and inquire about doing a dog-and-pony series of debates "beginning with Carnegie Hall," he wistfully beckoned.

This initiative led his wife and him to Buckley's home in Stamford, Connecticut, where Buckley took him out on his thirty-six-foot sailboat. He was astonished when Buckley handed him the wheel, guiding him on a course to the end of the harbor. By the time dinner was over, the weather had turned quite cold, but Mailer told his wife, Jeannie, to get on the back of his motorcycle, and they sped off toward Brooklyn.[96]

A few years later in May 1968, Mailer appeared as a guest on *Firing Line* where the two predictably locked horns on a number of issues. (Mailer would make, in total, three appearances.)

Mailer, the tough guy of American letters, sauntered through this vale of tears November 2007, having succumbed to acute renal failure a month after lung surgery.

As recounted by Buckley, critic Mel Lyman expressed a keen curiosity about the implications of their encounter:

> A few years later I had Mailer as a guest on *Firing Line*, and one critic was deeply inquisitive about the meaning of the engagement. 'Seeing Buckley and Mailer on the tube yesterday I can't get over it,' Mel Lyman wrote in the *New York Avatar*. 'The greatest representation of the two extremes I've seen in a long time. Conservative meets liberal, Right meets Left, before meets after. Buckley didn't know what the f--- Mailer was talking about, it just jammed his computer, he even had to resort to childish insults to try and keep up his

> end.' ("Norman Mailer decocts matters of the first philosophical magnitude from an examination of his own ordure, and I am not talking about his books,' I had said.)"

"Buckley is a computer," Lyman went on, according to Buckley's article:

> Mailer is a man. A man can only be categorized and computerized to a certain extent, the greater part of him lies out of definition. Greatness can be recognized only. That is why Buckley went all to pieces when Mailer spoke of the "greatness" he saw in Castro. Buckley could only see the un-American activities accredited to the man, Castro. He could only see him as far as he could define his actions. Mailer could look right at him, like a child, and see a great force, an inner strength, a fearlessness that had nothing to do with right or wrong.

"I love Buckley," this Mailer disciple wrote, "but he makes me very sad, he's completely mastered the art of living in prison, but Mailer's mastered the art of what you do after you get out, and Buckley doesn't even know there is an out."[95]

The retrospective of their bloody encounter in Chicago and on camera aside, Buckley had kinder things to say in memoriam for his complicated friend.

He wrote that the "towering" figure of Mailer created, quite simply, some of the "most beautiful metaphors in the English language," adding stalwartly that he stands by that judgment.

While both William F. Buckley and Norman Mailer were the product of Ivy League institutions—Yale and Harvard, respectively—their experiences in these bastions of higher learning propelled them, at least in part, in divergent ideological directions.

Yet, for all their differences, both men clearly valued intellectual rigor and independence, traits they sharpened during their academic years. Today, however, the very institutions that once cultivated that diversity of thought have become, in many cases, echo chambers for conformity.

If there were one single purpose of America's universities, it should be, their highest calling and mandate is a commitment to free inquiry and debate.

And that well of free inquiry has been perhaps irreversibly tainted by the pollutants of ideological partisanship.

For one point of contact, we look toward the University of Virginia. The old institution, ironically founded by one of the creators of the First Amendment, Thomas Jefferson, was the subject of a case study in April 2024, performed by the National Association of Scholars, which looked at ratios of conservative and liberal thought on the campus.

I don't want this book to descend into the cold, leaden language so characteristic of case studies. I only want to briefly cite what the study found: "political donations from the faculty and staff of the University of Virginia go almost exclusively to the Democratic Party."[94]

When combining faculty and staff, the ratio of Democratic to Republican (D) donations is 18:1. However, when separating the two groups, the ratio for faculty is 24:1 while for staff it's 16:1. Among the blue-collar staff donors identified, the D ratio is 11:8, which stands in stark contrast to the white-collar staff ratio of 17.5:1 and the faculty's 24:1 ratio.

Can you guess which side of the aisle has captured academia? I think perhaps you can.

The most surprising thing about this study must surely be how unsurprising its conclusions were.

In keeping with this statistical reality, we have seen an explosion of Marxist thought that will require some extensive theological surgery.

This intellectual corrosion has been happening just below the surface in America's academic institutions and exploded in full force over the last ten years.

The great Oliver North, along with fellow Marine co-authors David Goetsch and Archie Jones, expound on this quite brilliantly in their critique of these increasingly idiocratic (to borrow a Mike Judge term) centers of supposedly higher learning titled *American Gulags: Marxist Tyranny in Higher Education and What to Do About It*, which sustains a respectable amount of righteous indignation throughout its prose.

They write, aptly, "when [one] examines[s] the unaltered historical record, what becomes undeniably clear is that the United States of America was founded by Christians and built on a solid foundation of biblical principles and Christian values."[81]

Here, once again, Buckley showed great prescience in predicting the erosion of that foundation.

In my conversation with Rich Lowry, he reflected on Buckley's early critiques in *God and Man at Yale*, published way back in 1951, noting Buckley's concern was largely about professors not being sufficiently pro-capitalist. "It seems completely naive from today's perspective," Lowry observed, "but he was identifying the beginning of a larger trend, one that would become much more dire over time. Now, it's just a five-alarm fire."

By the end of his life, Buckley felt gratified by certain conservative triumphs, especially the victory in the Cold War, but he was equally dismayed by areas where conservatism had failed to make inroads. "He was highly distressed by the things we weren't able to check at all," Lowry said. One of those areas was what Buckley called "the playboy philosophy"—a term, while quaint today, reflected his deep concern over cultural hedonism. This was a battle Buckley felt conservatives "continuously lost ground."

Lowry also noted Buckley's deep, sometimes paradoxical loyalty to institutions like Yale. "Church was foundational to him," he remarked, "but Yale was extremely important too." Even as he criticized the university's ideological drift, Buckley remained "deeply loyal" to it. He loved the place, adored being in its intellectual environment, and cherished traditions like hosting the a cappella group The Whiffenpoofs at events. For Buckley, institutions were worth preserving no matter how much they might disappoint him.

It is in the spirit of those cultural and spiritual repatriations that Marxist sentiment, which would almost naturally proliferate in the absence of the Christian ethic as far as Buckley was concerned, gained ground in academia and the broader culture, now engulfing society in that "five-alarm fire."

Buckley saw the erosion of biblical principles as leaving a void that would inevitably be filled by ideologies hostile to individual liberty and free markets. For him, the fight was not merely political but profoundly moral and spiritual, an effort to preserve the nation's founding Christian ethos against the rising tide of secularism and collectivism. This conviction, deeply rooted in his worldview, shaped Buckley's lifelong crusade to defend Western civilization from what he saw as its internal decay.

"When the foundations are being destroyed, what can the righteous do?" exclaims Psalm 11:3. [Bible - 7]

But central to Marxism's ability to rage like a wildfire throughout academia has been the "notorious" ignorance of Americans, their ignorance of what Marxism is.

In short—and there will be more to say later—"Marxism," the authors explain, "is a socio political, socioeconomic theory purporting to create a Utopian society free of class distinctions."

The idea is, people contribute equally (another term we'll turn a critical eye to later) to society. This is where the devious Marxist line of "from each according to his ability and to each according to his need" intrudes. The problem, among others and as they explain, is these impulses run antithetical to human nature which is precisely why Marxism can never work.

Academia has conformed to these ideals and, ironically, contributed to a loss of purpose with lemming-like obedience, revising history in ways that undermine America, while true freedom vanishes, as fleeting as breath on a mirror.

It is those cultural deformities that must be addressed in order to smooth and pave the road to civility.

But these are weeds that have grown for far too long and have grown far too thick.

Let's turn our eyes to what has been called by many the "failed state" that is California.

It was back in 1992, when the University of California, Los Angeles, received a generous grant of $2 million courtesy of the National Endowment for the Humanities as well as the US Department of Education.

The aim of the money was to change what was taught at the university's history classes by changing the standards for the books used. Five years later, UCLA achieved this goal.

It's all captured by Pat Buchanan in *The Death of the West: How Dying Populations and Immigrant Invasions Imperil Our Country and Civilization*.

According to him, here are some of the names not seen in any of those books: Paul Revere, Alexander Graham Bell, Thomas Edison, or the Wright Brothers.

In what would be perversely amusing were it not so abysmally disheartening, let's note that the founding dates of the environment organization the Sierra Club as well as NOW (the National Organization for Women) are given—as is pointed out in *American Gulags*—"special significance."[81]

Further, George Washington's presidency isn't mentioned, nor is his famous farewell address.

It is one the great oddities of Western culture and America specifically where the US and her accomplishments are, to coin a phrase, evil-washed in her own history books.

That is, the United States is often treated as an evil empire or some sort of superpower with manifest destiny at the core of its motivations.

The good Colonel North and his company noticed this as well when they called out how UCLA had at least in one instance used a history book with one page on World War II.

The contents of that one page?

A few invidious lines of prose about the atomic bombs dropped on Hiroshima and Nagasaki. By all means shout out those sanguinary conflicts in the history books, but at the same time mention the attack on Pearl Harbor that precipitated the bombing, or perhaps the horrific Bataan Death March, or the dreaded Rape of Nanjing, all of which, far from being glossed over, aren't even mentioned.

Every country throughout history, certainly those with blood-stained misadventures of war, have their own butcher's bill to account for, and it seems that should be known to students of history.

But there are some other perhaps surprising and certainly notable examples of encroachment, most particularly and especially against Christians.

Colonel North and his crew point out a chilling intrusion on what we might think of as the self-evident right of freedom of speech and the axiomatic necessity to defend it.

It was at the State University of New York at Buffalo (SUNY) where a speech code was established that the book characterized as a "wolf in sheep's clothing" policy. That is always the form codified limits of freedom of speech typically take, isn't it?

This one was a policy that made, let's call it, unkind speech in residence halls impossible.

North, Goetsch, and Jones explain that with a policy of this kind, a student, perhaps a Christian one, who wished to exercise his own voice of dissent against another student's personal choices or behaviors could well be charged and disciplined.

They do make the philosophical hedge, of course. Universities can establish and maintain codes of conduct tending toward protecting students and their ability to sleep, to roam the hall, etc., but the form this code takes is a rather surreptitious and insidious way of stymieing the speech of others.

A policy such as this would very likely make Christians the "most frequent targets of speech code violations."

They also make the argument I myself have made in another context, which is along the lines of "Who gets to decide which speech is harmful?"

An extremely important point. To whom do we designate the right to decide which speech is harmful and who is the harmful speaker? This right can't just be assumed, though there will always be those who will kindly assume it on our behalf.

Always beware of those who proclaim, in policy form, they have your best interests at heart.

It is not fanatical to observe that such proclamations carry the unmistakable reek of the totalitarian temptation.

It was even worse in Pennsylvania where a Christian student was silenced by Temple University for witnessing for his faith. The student, who by the way was also a member of the Pennsylvania National Guard, was prohibited from making Christian or indeed conservative-oriented statements to his fellow students. No doubt Buckley would have brought this to the attention of the *National Review* faithful.

They cite a third instance, among others, where two students at the Georgia Institute of Technology were treated to a hearty helping of "religious discrimination" simply for maintaining the Christian worldview regarding homosexuality. This view—which was simply a view; it wasn't a hate crime or anything of the like—supposedly encroached on the institute's Safe Space training policy, which as Colonel North points out was openly hostile to religions that didn't accept homosexuality.

For those curious about the outcome, the resultant lawsuit saw to the removal of the discriminatory religious information from the program's training manual, finding Georgia Tech officials "violated the Establishment Clause by favoring one religion over another in the state-associated Safe Space Program."

Aside from this active aggression toward the Christian ethic, there is also, simply, the unmitigated danger of the stupidity undergirding it.

This stupidity is clearly—on the verge of blindingly—presented by those who espouse, not to say impose, Marxism in their refusal to think critically and to turn an angry eye to those who do.

Just to put a point on it so it doesn't seem like I am playing word games, if someone isn't capable of critical thinking, what else can we designate that person other than stupid? It seems to me the classification intrudes on its own.

Here are some partial renderings, courtesy of the *American Gulags* authors, of the clear and present tactics of such a Marxist-leaning individual.

A current favorite is introducing irrelevant information, commonly referred to as a strawman. The Marines reference a hypothetical debate with someone of the Marxist ilk arguing the Second Amendment should be done away with since the founding fathers couldn't have known of the firepower brought on by, say, an AK-47. This is irrelevant because the extent of the firepower bears not at all on the right, enshrined in that glorious amendment. Indeed, the whole point of the passage is to allow a well-regulated militia among the citizenry in case of, and especially in response to, government tyranny.

A personal favorite logical fallacy to notice, which the authors dwell upon as well, is that of arguing from ignorance. These are people who really should understand how their own "arguments" sound when they are played back to them. If nothing else, they certainly deserve that.

Submitted for your consideration, dear reader, is an imagined discussion about serving in the military. One college student says, "I will never serve in the military. All they do is teach you how to kill innocent women and children." One who is bound by the chains of logic and sound reasoning will feel obliged to point out the miasma of ignorance clouding that student's entire proposition.

The person in question has never served in the military and thus has no basis for arguing the claim.

Buckley can also assist here with a favored thought experiment he posed often. This was in regard to how to honestly discuss certain topics. He said if there is an instance of one man who pushes an old lady out of the way of oncoming traffic and there is another who rather happily pushes an old lady into the way of oncoming traffic, the way to absolutely not have an intellectual romp on the matter would be to frame it as discussing people who like to push old ladies.

We must not leapfrog over the favorite or at least most noticeable tactic of Marxists (I don't mind simply saying leftists), that of the ever-illuminating ad hominem attack. Not illuminating because it shines light on the subject at hand but illuminating in how much it reveals about the person performing it.

In short, it means one who attacks the person and not the argument.

American Gulags cites specifically the case of a California professor—not a student, a *professor*—who referred to Johnathan Lopez, who was a student at Los Angeles City College, as a "fascist b_____d."[81]

The great sin committed in that instance was to argue in favor of traditional marriage.

As a relevant aside, Lopez sued the Los Angeles Community College District after claiming the professor discriminated against him for his Christian beliefs during a classroom presentation.

But the fallacy lurking under, just barely under, the surface of this particular mode of argument is so blatant and self-evident, I would only serve to insult you by offering any further analysis.

There are a slew of other bad faith-laden syllogisms on offer from Marxists and leftists, but that would well comprise its own book.

It should be said, before I sound like too much of an idealogue, the Right and conservatives, particularly in today's polarized climate, are just as capable of stifling their own critical thinking as the Left.

You've heard this before as well. Too quick or too reflexive a resort to conservative-flavored ex-communications such as referring to people who disagree as "sheeple." Or they become enamored with any number of bizarre conspiracy theories which don't exactly engender goodwill, such as adrenochrome or Pizzagate. Not exactly the height of intellectual seriousness or honesty.

But if, for instance, someone were to have their doubts about whether a private citizen should have access to say, an AR-15, given the litany of horrific mass shootings we have seen, the reflex of the Right too often is "This person is a fascist who seeks to rescind the rights of others" rather than giving the argument due intellectual consideration.

The point here is, we should apply the same standard we do in the legal domain. Just as we presume innocence until guilt is proven, we should presume good faith until it's proven beyond a reasonable doubt the person is sullied by the mud of bad faith. The good news is, one can ascertain this quite quickly by way of engagement.

As we've seen through the cases of Johnathan Lopez and other students across the country, censorship and discrimination can come in many forms. Whether it's a professor silencing a Christian student, a policy favoring certain religious views, or even conservatives engaging in their own brand of bad-faith arguments, the real danger lies in the erosion of dialogue.

A staggering example of the intellectual suicide so prevalent on college campuses springs forth to us from the University of Kansas in October 2024.

It was Professor Phillip Lowcock who, while bloviating and virtue-signaling to his class about the "serious problems" going on with men who think guys are smarter than girls, clearly had a thought that was father to his wish. This was, by the way, when he was knowingly being recorded in class, which would lead one to wonder what he wishes in private.

"There are going to be some males in our society that will refuse to vote for a potential female president because they don't think females are smart enough to be president," he pontificated.

And yes, of course, he was referring to the upcoming election between then-Vice President Kamala Harris and Donald Trump.

"We could line all those guys up and shoot them. They clearly don't understand the way the world works."

It seemed this was the real and true Professor Lowcock coming to bear. You may accuse me of assassinating his character, but it seems his character committed suicide a long time ago.

He tried his best to backpedal by adding, "Did I say that? Scratch that from the recording," he added. "I don't want the deans hearing that I said that."[14]

Apart from wondering how a lecturer in the Health, Sport, and Exercise Sciences department at KU would start to wander onto the political landscape during a speech—which likely requires its own examinations and prescriptions by the way—one sees a clear, proud, and above all tribal alliance to a certain political persuasion.

Now, let's be fair. The professor was, at the time of this writing, suspended, and KU apologized on his behalf, which of course amounts to an apology not worth giving and even less worth hearing.

But this commitment to intellectual laziness and stupidity rears its ugly head still further with the surreptitious intellectual erasure of those who have contributed to Western thought.

Sharpening the point, Douglas Murray gives account, once again in *War on the West*, of having mentioned in passing the philosopher Immanuel Kant during a talk, of course, at an American university.

When taking questions, one student approached the microphone and asked Murray if he was aware Kant was known for barking out the N-word.

Aside from working out how likely it would have been for a German in the 18th century to be attached to the word-that-must-not-be-said, Murray also tried to cement in his mind why the question was worth asking, let alone answering.

New York Post contributor opines about the ever-growing cultural sentiment that if one can say (however inaccurately) that Kant used the N-word, one is thus excused from paying Kant any mind whatsoever.[13]

In this sense, one no longer needs to trouble oneself with plowing through Kant's *The Metaphysics of Morals*, for instance. Simply label him a racist and then get on with the grander project of sneering at those you may learn from.

Now, I hold no particular brief for Immanuel Kant, one of the larger influences on Marx, but take that narcotic habit of burlesquing people as racists and think of all the intellectual roads you would sidestep in favor of a world of idiotic and tribal bliss.

This habit, at scale in society, is a sure recipe for its degradation and—to resort to a fashionable term—cancellation.

Buckley's favorite book calls out to us through the mists of history from Proverbs 1:7 that ". . . fools despise wisdom and instruction." [Bible - 8]

We must be vigilant against the forces seeking to quash free expression no matter where they come from. This isn't just about the Left or the Right; it's about preserving the marketplace of ideas. The ability to debate, to question, and to disagree is at the heart of our constitutional republic. When that is lost—whether through institutional mandates or self-imposed echo chambers—our society becomes impoverished and, worse, it becomes dangerous.

In the end, the true test of a culture's intellectual health lies not in how it handles agreeable ideas but in how it responds to dissent. It's time to demand more than hollow, often performative, rhetoric from both sides of the ideological spectrum and instead to strive for genuine engagement rooted in respect, logic, and the courage to listen.

That is precisely how William F. Buckley would have wanted it: a society where ideological differences are confronted with reason, not vitriol; where respect for opposing views is not only tolerated but encouraged; and where the principles of faith and intellect meet in the service of a higher, more civil public discourse.

CHAPTER 4

Christopher Hitchens: From Debate to Admiration

Percy Bysshe Shelley famously wrote poets are, "the unacknowledged legislators of the world." In one sense perhaps, only in parochial and provincial terms, Buckley has been greatly unacknowledged for his influence in bringing to the American cultural conscience a public intellectual who, paradoxically but yet still true to form, had political and ideological leanings polar opposite of his own. It would seem Buckley most preferred to focus on the intersection between the literary calling and the public responsibility.

To that end, it should be known the ironically venerated journalist, author, and infamous atheist Christopher Hitchens made several appearances on *Firing Line*.

Bill Buckley's son, also named Christopher, confirmed in an exclusive interview that Hitch, with whom his father was friends for over thirty years, relayed to him that his father gave him his "first significant exposure on American television."

What irony that the endlessly pious figure of Buckley, who has been known as the St. Paul of the conservative movement, played such a role in helping to launch arguably the most fiery atheist of the 20th century!

Hitchens, despite his socialist, Marxist, and of course, antitheistic worldview, was quite fond of Buckley but often found the possibility of slinging his arm over Buckley's shoulder with the intention of sauntering gleefully to a nearby bar impossible.

In a cut interview for the acclaimed Buckley-Vidal documentary, *Best of Enemies*, Hitchens ruminated on how "it used to strike me with William Buckley that he was . . . a slightly insecure person. I say that only because if at the end of the taping of *Firing Line*, which I frequently did with him at his request, I would say, 'Well, do you have time for a cocktail before the next show or before the next appointment?' he would always have to be running and diving into a car, or catching a plane, or going to a book signing."

"So he seemed," Hitchens went on, "to arrange his life so that there was very little privacy or time for intimacy or informality in it. You had the feeling that he was repressing the demons that would close in on him if he was left alone with his own thoughts or with someone who was only there to chat. Wasn't there to interview him or ask him questions."[15]

While the possibility of a close friendship may have been made difficult, there was no question the two were fond of, if not at the very least held an admiration for, each other.

Christopher Hitchens made five separate appearances on *Firing Line* over the course of four years. This would include one *Firing Line* debate and one instance where he held the ever-rotating mantle of examiner to inquire about the Contra movements in Nicaragua.

One memorable appearance took place back in 1984. The title was "Is there a liberal crack-up?" and it concerned R. Emmett Tyrrell's *The Liberal Crack-Up*, so it was the conservative Tyrrell, the "radical" liberal Hitchens, and, of course, Buckley.

The book was built on the premise the liberal movement was a failure, and it was that motion which the three were meant to discuss.

Tyrrell did seem to display throughout a "want of gallantry" not just for women or the women's movement, which was discussed, but he also seemed to have a bizarre allergy to being disagreed with.

It seemed to be nothing but ad hominem attack (and lazy ones at that) with tinges of an inexplicable confidence that those ad-hom assaults would carry the debate for him.

Conversely or perhaps paradoxically, Hitchens and Buckley, despite their obvious conflicts of ideals, seemed right at home debating each other. One could, in fact, easily imagine that, particularly with Hitchens, their conversation would have happily been picked up at cocktail hour at a nearby bar without the corrosive element of Tyrrell's shenanigans. The punchline here is Buckley's unwillingness to give his focus to the person who presumably agreed with him on much more than Hitchens did.

Here, Buckley would perhaps invoke the lessons of 1 Samuel 16:7, "The Lord does not look at the things people look at. People look at the outward appearance, but the Lord looks at the heart." [Bible - 9] There is far more that defines a person than just their political views. This was a value Buckley knew well and lived by.

The two also made a joint appearance on Dartmouth-man Peter Robinson's program *Uncommon*

Knowledge for a retrospective on the sixties. If the curious viewer had the program muted, it would have looked like a friendly chat between old friends. Remarkable considering one was a radical Catholic conservative and the other, an atheistic Marxist socialist.

It is also well worth noting, both Hitchens and Buckley were intellectually honest enough to admit what they both got wrong in the sixties. For Buckley, it was his support of the Vietnam War and venturing to the wrong side of the civil rights debate, positions he had since changed. Hitchens, for his part, regretted some of the hedonistic excesses of the sixties.

Buckley must have had at least the trace of a soft spot for the *God Is Not Great: How Religion Poisons Everything* author, since Buckley invited Hitchens to take part in the last *Firing Line* debate of the show's run.

It was in Oxford, Mississippi, 1999, when Hitchens took part in a panel debate. Motion on the floor: *Resolved: The Federal Government Should Not Impose a Tax on Electronic Commerce.*

Don't forget, dear reader, there was a time at the advent of online selling when the issue of e-commerce taxation was a hotly debated and controversial topic.

In his opening statement, Hitchens thanked *Firing Line* and thus Buckley for the "bruising education in Libertarian and Conservative values."[16]

The gratitude was not typical Hitchens-flavored irony either. He meant it. He often said that most of what he knew as a commentator and debater (he as well as Buckley are often mentioned in the same breath when one considers the great debaters of the twentieth century), he learned from talking with people whom he disagreed with, often quite aggressively.

Hitchens kept his own stable of ideologically opposite friends throughout his life, which included the former head of the National Institute of Health, Dr. Francis

Collins, and the highly regarded Christian apologist Dinesh D'Souza among many others.

His friend and frequent debating antagonist, the Calvinist preacher Douglas Wilson, relayed to me in my interview with him some years back how he marveled at Hitch's willingness to take his "atheist screed" (his polemic *God Is Not Great*) to the Bible Belt and beyond for a series of debates with many apologists, Wilson among them. Wilson greatly admired that Hitchens "didn't want to have a wine and cheese party release of the book where a bunch of fellow atheists in Manhattan congratulate him. He released the book with a general invitation to debate all comers."

That signals a deep thirst for knowledge on Hitchens's part. He, as well as Buckley, always seemed to be hungrily operating on the margins of a potentially rich harvest of future knowledge and wisdom. A lesson for all of us today, to be sure, as well as a warning against the wisdom-allergen of tribalism.

While Hitchens and Buckley did not share the deep friendship Buckley with figures like John Kenneth Galbraith or Murray Kempton, Hitchens did address Buckley's intellectual approach in a 2007 interview on C-SPAN's *In Depth*, when a caller asked him to categorize it.

The longtime columnist for *The Nation* answered with uncharacteristic warmth, "Mr. Buckley was incredibly good to me when he was running *Firing Line* . . . and would have me on quite often."[17] Hitchens elaborated with a comment that not only spoke to Buckley's ethic as a TV host but to his entire ethic as an ardent Christian living the values of tolerance and good faith, in both senses of the term:

> I remember thinking with *Firing Line*, unlike a lot of debate shows on TV, if you left that studio

> thinking, "Damn, I wished I remembered to make this point or make this point that way," it was your fault; you had every chance to do it. No one was trying to hurry you up, or shut you down, or cut you off.[17]
>
> I am grateful to him for that style and the style in which, for the most part, he ran *National Review*."

That is quite an extraordinary thing to hear from the man who openly excoriated the Catholic Church for the Crusades, injustices toward women, and the burning alive in the main square of Prague the great Czech Protestant Jan Huss, among a library of other grievances.

This was on top of being a vituperative critic of Mary Teresa Bojaxhiu, the woman known to us historically as Mother Teresa, whom Buckley revered and who prompted Hitchens's writing of the impolitely titled polemic *The Missionary Position: Mother Teresa in Theory and Practice*.

This certainly isn't to suggest Buckley wasn't above anger if his sensibilities were infringed upon. That would be a bit much to ask. Indeed Christopher Buckley remembers, upon seeing Hitchens's well-known attack on the woman styling herself as Mother Teresa, his father wrote a note on top of the mailed Xerox of *The Nation* piece to his producer (presumably Warren Steibel) a venomous editorial order: "I never want to lay eyes on this guy again."[18]

But even there, his Christian virtue of forgiveness peeks through his actions as the emerging sun overlooks the hill at dawn.

His father "tolerated pretty much anything except attacks on his beloved Catholic Church and its professors," the *Thank You for Smoking* author revealed.[18]

Nonetheless, Buckley, the father, simply "couldn't help but forgive."

"Did you see the piece on Chirac by your friend Hitchens in the *Journal* today?" he said one day, with a smile and an admiring sideways shake of the head. "Absolutely devastating!"[18]

The following year, after Buckley's death, Hitchens penned a reflective piece on Buckley that could be described as a critical (what else would one expect from the man who directed fiery critiques at the Almighty Himself?) love letter which echoed Kempton's refrain on Buckley's "genius at friendships." He noted, "Buckley was willing to be immensely friendly with figures from the gay Right, such as the doomed congressman Bob Bauman of Maryland or the flamboyant Marvin Liebman."[19]

Hitchens continued to remark, "Bill's gift for friendship with some liberals—John Kenneth Galbraith most notably—was the counterpart of his challenge to their monopoly on the word 'intellectual.'"[19]

The liberal radical-turned-independent closed by remembering, "William F. Buckley Jr. was never solemn except or unless on purpose, and seldom if ever flippant where witty would do, and in saying this, I hope I pay him the just tribute that is due to a serious man."[19]

Here, we must do our own reflecting on the obvious respect the two famous polemicists held for each other. Perhaps Buckley would invoke the admonishment revealed in 1 Peter 3:8: "Be like-minded, be sympathetic, love one another, be compassionate and humble." [Bible - 10] Despite their fierce debates, Buckley and his counterpart demonstrated that true understanding and respect can, in fact, extend across ideological divides and be rooted in shared humanity. That seems to be all but forgotten in today's society.

This is by no means exclusive to, say, the Twitter (X)-verse. Political officers up to and including President Biden have perhaps forgotten shared humanity regarding those who happen to support Donald Trump. It was in 2023 the White House warned, "This MAGA threat is the threat to the brick and mortar of our democratic institutions. But it's also a threat to the character of our nation and gives our—that gives our Constitution life, that binds us together as Americans in common cause."[20]

But since neither Left nor Right win expiation under scrutiny, Donald Trump's office put out in 2023 that "crooked Joe Biden" had weaponized the Department of Homeland Security, and "will continue to expand its efforts to 'fight election interference,' which authority the DHS has used to massively interfere with our elections and our democracy," so neither side is guiltless in casting aspersions.[21]

One notices when the two met to debate in 2024, neither seemed keen to bring up their various points to the others, which cements at least in this author's mind that the horrible performative quality so often pervasive in politicians these days reared its ugly head in both cases.

How we yearn for a time when we could simply debate respectfully and indeed "be compassionate and humble." The radical Catholic right-winger and the Marxist antitheist Hitchens were clearly grateful for the chance at an intellectual tête-à-tête.

In many ways, it seemed in Buckley's time the two political sides were grateful for the existence of the other as means to perpetually refine their own arguments. Such is the dialectic of debate.

The surplus value on offer to a culture embracing gratitude was by no means foreign to Buckley.

After all, it was in 1990 he published a book, one of his more underrated ones in my judgment, called, aptly, *Gratitude: Reflections on What We Owe Our Country.*

Buckley wrote in a stirring display of prescience given the depths to which our culture has sunk, "the instability of family life, listlessness at school" coupled with what he termed a "growing national tendency to corruption, or hedonism" as well as a "callousness that breeds ugliness of behavior" are in large part symptoms of one's "failure to acknowledge a running debt to one's homeland."[22]

Buckley thought the ethic of gratitude should be adopted and folded into, if not public policy, at least the cultural ethos.

What he proposed, somewhat daringly, was a kind of voluntary draft into national public service in a showcase of gratitude for the incredible benefits (you won't get me to say *privileges*) endemic to being born on or moving to American soil.

In summary, Buckley advocated that American citizens contribute a year of public service of some kind to their country in the spirit of gratefulness for, say, the freedom of speech, which is a uniquely Western value.

In a *Booknotes* discussion with Brian Lamb, Buckley expounded on this idea and its social utility.

It was the lack of any appreciation for what we get for nothing that prompted the idea. And that appreciation could be channeled into one year's service. The service could be, as Buckley explained to the CSPAN founder, a year's service helping people in hospitals, helping to teach children who couldn't read, and helping with the environment, for instance.[23]

Once again, it would not have been mandatory and wouldn't have taken the same form as, say, military conscription into the army, as forced displays of gratitude rather misses the point entirely, but Buckley very much wanted to assist in "helping an ethos materialize."[23]

Buckley did pose the thoughtful ideal that institutions such as Harvard embraced this as a social policy and, for instance, withholding permission to apply for financial aid from students who have not taken up this movement toward gratitude.

"If Harvard would do it, then everybody else would do it eventually."[23]

Perhaps our culture today could do with a dose of gratitude as well.

The national ethos today does seem to be an orientation toward ingratitude as well as a loss of a sense of duty, which would follow axiomatically.

To tackle the prevalence of ingratitude first, notice the opposite of gratitude—resentment—has reared its ugly head and doubled and perhaps tripled since the advent of social media.

It used to be prior to, say, 2005, we only had proper peeks into the life of how many people? Twenty? Maybe twenty-five? There was just the actuarial reality: one simply didn't know enough people to be overtaken by jealousy and thus a degree of resentment.

There amounts to a massive confidence blow lurking beneath the surface. After all, if one only knew, say, twenty-five people, one was more or less guaranteed to be the best of that group at something.

Now, thanks to social media, everyone is in everyone else's tribe, if only by way of comparison and that age-old effort of "keeping up with the Joneses."

Also, I don't think it runs the risk of being an overstatement or even controversial at all to point out that social media provides only the most flattering glimpses into the lives of others.

The net result is the crippling feeling that no one is as good as anyone else. And we wonder why the proliferation of social media has so destroyed the mental health of so many, particularly young people, in the world.

But also, paradoxically, ingratitude seems to creep in with excess. There is no doubt America is the greatest country in the world. Even those who claim to despise it—one has to notice—tend to stick around.

America is so great, often its supposed denigrated denizens have to manufacture their own oppression. And one can think of their own favorite examples of this.

This manufactured oppression, paired with the endless "compare and despair" attitude fostered by social media, has led to a dangerous dialectical cocktail of entitlement and dissatisfaction. Instead of appreciating the unprecedented opportunities and freedoms life in America offers, we've become fixated on superficial grievances and imaginary slights, which have given way to fanaticism and thus proliferated tribalism.

This constant exposure to others' highlights leaves many feeling inferior or persecuted even when they're among the most privileged. In a society as prosperous as ours, it seems that real gratitude has been displaced by the need to adopt victimhood, and the effects on our collective psyche are profound.

There is also a nefarious theological problem to shine a light on here. It seems since any scintilla of God, even the mention of the name—and forget reverence—has in many ways become anathema in society today. It isn't any great wonder narcissism, along with a heaping dose of nihilism, is creeping into the cultural zeitgeist. But it's an emaciation of gratitude and an obesity of resentment that are the activating factors.

"People of resentment," Douglas Murray wrote in *The War on the West*, "are intent on forbidding the best emotions."[13] The best emotion, the opposite of resentment, surely must be gratitude.

Murray puts it beautifully when he writes aptly, "Without some sense of gratitude, it is impossible to get anything into any proper order."[13]

Buckley was a man whose incredible zest for life, coupled with his enormous accomplishments, revealed his deep sense of gratitude.

He went to an Ivy League school (we'll forgive him for that), he was a CIA agent, he founded the modern conservative movement, he took the helm of what would become the longest running program with a single host in American television history, he founded an influential magazine which still influences to this day, he spoke three languages (English was his third language, by the way, after Spanish and French), he played several instruments, and he sailed the Atlantic and Pacific Oceans. As if that weren't enough, he became a best-selling spy-novelist, penning more than eleven of his Blackford Oakes novels.

In many ways, Buckley's achievements were an expression of something deeper than mere ambition and, yes, the means to do so. They were manifestations of his gratitude for the opportunities and gifts he was afforded. He didn't merely seek success for its own sake; his was a life lived with a profound sense of purpose, driven by an acknowledgment of the blessings bestowed upon him. Whether sailing across oceans, debating intellectual adversaries, or crafting novels, Buckley's gratitude was always present, fueling his relentless pursuit of both adventure and truth. This sense of gratitude, however, is precisely what seems to be eroding in society today, giving way to resentment.

On resentment, the Bible reminds us in Ephesians 4:31 to "get rid of all bitterness, rage and anger, brawling and slander, along with every form of malice." [Bible - 3] On the sunnier point of gratitude, Colossians 3:15 calls us to "let the peace of Christ rule in your hearts, since as members of one body you were called to peace. And be thankful." [Bible - 4]

So, whatever one's religious fealty, know the Bible and the Christian ethic, as Buckley assuredly would have pointed out, do prescribe a helpful immunization against the narcissism and nihilism that have so come to preoccupy society—and may the principles Buckley lived out stimulate our national ethos toward a more civil way of communicating, a more grateful way of living.

CHAPTER 5

Murray Kempton: Intellectual Companionship

One might get the impression a presumably prudish or straight laced man such as William F. Buckley may have been someone who took everything in his life seriously. He may be someone who has no understanding of, let alone a capacity for, wit or risibility. This would very slightly but crucially misrepresent him.

He often refused to take himself too seriously. Back in 1968, Buckley appeared on a show with famed comedian Woody Allen. There, the untrained observer of Buckley might have been taken aback by two things. The first is Buckley's aforementioned though not nearly mentioned enough sense of humor. He was able to comedically spar with Allan to the delight of the audience. In fact, the facility of humor was one he deployed on a consistent basis on *Firing Line*, so if the passive observer is astonished by Buckley's wit, it would have to be mostly their fault.

The second would probably be Buckley's ability to laugh at himself. Allen made a couple joking comments poking fun at Buckley which he seemed to happily take in stride and return in kind.

These traits would have fit snugly with the disposition of Murray Kempton and therefore fairly easily fostered a deeply rewarding friendship. Kempton was a man who, echoing Buckley somewhat, said he would never seek a job at *The New York Times* as they commit the egregious and unforgivable sin of taking themselves far too seriously. If this wasn't enough of a bond, Kempton was a fervent anticommunist.

After all, David Remnick of *The New Yorker* would later write, "Kempton was nearly alone in championing men and women who had fallen under the spell of ideology and the Communist Party and never seemed to cease paying for their folly." In one episode of *Firing Line*, on which Kempton was a guest, Buckley opened by saying "Murray Kempton is the finest writer in the newspaper profession," so one could see right away the respect Buckley showed to Kempton. This is fairly fertile ground for a blossoming friendship. For Buckley, the liberal Pulitzer Prize—winning journalist was a perfect ideological and intellectual foil.

The two seemed to attack ideas in the same way as well. In his autobiography *Miles Gone By*, Buckley wrote, Kempton "lacerated us all, but scorned only the hypocrites and the arrogant."[24] That is the perfect descriptor of someone intent on attacking the idea and not the person. It was in this spirit Buckley and Kempton soldiered on in their relationship.

Within six months of *National Review's* arrival on the political scene in 1955, there were three left-leaning magazines more than willing to offer their critiques in print. One was *Harper's Magazine*; the second was *Commentary*.

The third was called, aptly, *The Progressive.* In it, a piece written by none other than Kempton points to the sheer boredom-inducing prose that pervaded the new magazine. It was rather appropriately titled "Buckley's National Bore." Worse than that, the Pulitzer Prize—winning journalist wrote that this supposedly revivified conservative movement is most bootable for its already advanced "state of wither."[25]

It will come as no surprise Buckley had his own wit-laced barb at the ready for a counter-attack in print.

"How can one reasonably expect a magazine, written and edited by mortals, to arrest something far gone in putrefaction and bring it back to life?"

The idea of the full circle is a wonderful trope reverberating throughout human drama. The idea of a resolution is, by intuition and not by analysis, immensely satisfying.

Imagine, then, the fount of exuberance and satisfaction springing forth from Buckley when, twenty years later, he received a personal letter from Kempton asserting (not merely admitting, which would be enough) he "would like to do a piece a month somewhere that is just rumination. . . . Candidly, yours is the only editorial mind and *NR*'s curiously the only temper with which I could conceive myself as fitting. Would it be possible?"[25]

Thus, the admittedly short-lived column sprang forth from of Kempton's typewriter, "Thoughts Astray," was borne. It perhaps only four times graced the pages of *National Review* before Kempton moved on to his next conquest.[25]

When Buckley published his famous polemic *Up from Liberalism* in 1959, Kempton unsurprisingly had thoughts to conjure and words to write. The book was a scathing critique, amounting to a full-throated repudiation of liberal ideology. As its title suggests, Buckley urged the reader to guide their gaze and political fealty up from liberalism toward what he would describe as "political realism."

So, it was in the 1960 February issue of *Commentary* Kempton published his review of the book. But even in criticism, there was an inordinate amount of civility, burgeoning on friendliness, sprinkled throughout the piece. He wrote lovingly:

> I never think of Buckley without affection and rarely do I think of him without a cloudy memory of one of the Winston Churchill anecdotes. Mr. Churchill was sitting through an especially tedious speech in the House when his eye fell upon an elder member who leaned forward holding up his ear trumpet, the better to hear the speaker. "And who," Mr. Churchill asked, "is that fool disregarding his natural advantages?"[26]

John Avlon wrote in *National Review* that Kempton was, in Buckley's own words, "a socialist—a sworn enemy of all anti-Communist legislation, sworn friend of militant unionism." He also, according to Buckley, attacked the written word with characteristic wit and irony and a compassion which is sometimes unruly. More to the point, he was "a great artist and a great friend."[27]

The two came into contact when the editor of *Monocle Quarterly* came to Buckley with the idea that he do a profile on Kempton for the magazine's first issue. Here's what Buckley recalled:

> [I] told the editor that the assignment was too burdensome, given that Kempton wrote three columns every week and had been doing so for ten years—there was no way I could do a comprehensive analysis of his writing and his views. What

> I would agree to undertake, under the stress of raw economy, was an essay based on the columns by Murray Kempton published in the three weeks before I wrote.[27]

Buckley expounded on this in his book *Cruising Speed: A Documentary*:,

> How to do a piece which even attempts to survey Murray Kempton's work? I hit on the device of writing "A Fortnight with Murray Kempton." I took eight consecutive columns by Murray, the eight that were published immediately before I embarked on the project. The essay was successful, I thought, because its limitations were at once explicit and modest. I allowed myself to meander as I thought it was useful.[28]

When Buckley famously decided to run against liberal Republican (the less-than-kind among us would likely use the term *RINO* now) John Lindsay, Kempton certainly had, at times, been of two minds on the matter. First, he was an ardent and unapologetic supporter of Lindsay. In fact, Lindsay proudly displayed a campaign poster directly quoting Kempton when he said of Lindsay, "He is fresh and everyone else is tired." However, Kempton also admired the fact that Buckley didn't actually plan on doing a great deal of campaigning.

At a press conference following his announcement, Buckley explained he did not anticipate engaging in much campaigning due to his other obligations. Kempton found this reassuring, noting how Buckley preferred to focus on his work rather than campaign during business hours in contrast to other incumbents who used taxpayer funds for electioneering.

Buckley admitted he disliked campaigning, even going so far as to call it "streetwalking," considering it vulgar and beneath him. He made it clear he would not partake in what he viewed as performative gestures, stating, "I will not go to Irish centers and go dancing. I will not go to Jewish centers and eat blintzes, nor will I go to Italian centers and pretend to speak Italian."

Instead, Buckley preferred to release thoughtfully crafted position papers and engage in debates with reporters. Among the proposals he offered, one that generated significant attention, was his suggestion to build a bikeway from 125th Street to 1st Street.

So, even when there was direct opposition and a real potential bulwark against an ever-blossoming friendship, their mutual affection endured.

Mr. Kempton made no fewer than five *Firing Line* appearances. The first aired June 6, 1966. It was titled "Bobby Kennedy and Other Mixed Blessings." The central thrust of the discussion was Kennedy's rampant attacking of Lyndon Johnson. Immediately apparent throughout the conversation was the mutual affection the two men shared. There was some gentle sparring over Bobby Kennedy and the visibility of unions, but any disagreement was absent malice and ill-intent. Indeed, if a viewer was not paying proper attention, it might well look (just as with Hitchens) as if the two were casually agreeing with each other the entire episode.

True to form, the episode ended with Kempton pointing admiringly to an article on Senator Kennedy that Buckley wrote about two weeks prior. In the article, Buckley said one of Kennedy's great strengths was, nothing he can do really seems to hurt him.

Kempton went on record and out of his way to say he completely agreed with Buckley on that point. It does seem, it is this humility in the face of potential disagreement and the willingness to concede the points that should be conceded in a debate that we would refer to as *coming into the argument in good faith*. This is precisely the impulse, nurtured at least in part by Buckley's Catholic disposition, that should be resuscitated and revitalized in contemporary political discussions if indeed they must be had, which they typically don't.

Kempton's second and third *Firing Line* appearances was a two-parter titled "What's Ahead for the Democrats?" in 1984. There was special consideration given to the topic because the Democratic National Convention was less than a month away. Both episode airings were a smattering of various political positions. Not incidentally, doesn't it say quite a lot that so many Democrats and Republicans were eager to sit down to seriously discuss and debate one another? An efflorescence of this not-so-regnant impulse has unthinkable levels of benefit to society and culture in the current age.

Along with the liberal Kempton and the of course considerably less liberal Buckley, there was one other representative of the Democrats: Mark Green.

Mr. Green was a mainstay on Ralph Nader's campaign for ten years and would go on to host a nationally syndicated radio show. In the Republican corner, along with Buckley, was Richard Brookhiser, a senior contributor to *National Review*.

On March 28, 1994, almost three decades after his first appearance on *Firing Line*, Kempton appeared for an episode that didn't have any agenda whatsoever, all but ensuring a fairly chaotic but likely entertaining conversation. It was called, simply, "Ruminations with Murray Kempton."

Although Kempton and Buckley disagreed on public policy most of the time, their exchanges were marked by cordiality, with no tension despite their differing views.

Kempton observed, through hosting his own program that Buckley became acquainted with many more people, including figures who had a criminal past, and yet Buckley managed to discern honor in some while recognizing its absence in others. "There are very few people who have honor," Kempton remarked.

Buckley, in turn, reflected on his life philosophy: "The great aim of life is to have as few apologies to make as humanly possible." He also shared a memory from the McCarthy Era, stating, "The only terror I felt... was from liberals who used to yell at me for being seen in public talking to Roy Cohn."

Although their conversation lacked a fixed agenda, Kempton's book, *Rebellions, Perversities, and Main Events*, which recapped some of his best columns, became a key talking point. In the book, Kempton offered high praise for Buckley, describing his "genius at friendships that surpass all understanding."[29]

Buckley responded by quoting Norman Mailer, who praised Kempton's book, calling him "one of the very few American journalists in all our history to give life and depth to the way we think."

It was May 5, 1997, when Mr. Kempton finally succumbed to a long battle with pancreatic cancer. He was seventy-nine years old and, according to the *Washington Examiner*, "he wrote somewhere around 10,000 columns and scores of essays for the *New Republic* and the *New York Review of Books*"[30] and thus boasted a level of literary volume that might well rival Buckley's.

Buckley wrote:

> My own reaction, on hearing the news, was the spastic it's-for-the-best. I had a friend who took two bad years to yield, finally, to that affliction. Ten days before Murray died, lying, white-haired

> and emaciated with a tube or two in his arm, he said, "Do you know what my medical expenses have been?—me, without any claim to any value in the free market? Three hundred thousand dollars!" I whistled, and shared, with Murray's son David, noisy and indignant astonishment at so gross a figure for eleven weeks' care.[24]
>
> He went on:
>
> Without exactly delving into the question of resources, the conversation proceeded on the assumption (generally safe, though not always) that somebody, somewhere, would handle the cost of the illness, however long it lasted. Whatever the clinical prospects there was no impulse in that little room by the Hudson River on 87th Street to pack it all in.[24]
>
> In 1995 Murray's wife, Beverly had died after a long ordeal. He wrote to me, "I'm sure you have no end of those dear friends, Job's counselors, who describe the worst things as for the best as if to congratulate you for release from inconveniences. The day before she died one such reminded me that it might be better, and I was grateful for the impulse that welled up and impelled me to reply that my views are the Pope's and we both prefer life to death.[24]

For Buckley, Murray Kempton was a worthy political sparring partner but an even more worthwhile friend. In their several-decade friendship, they had many civil but nonetheless charged discussions. One thing they always remembered to do—and this might be the perfect parting but by no means exhaustive call to action in the name of contemporary civility—was to not take each other or themselves too seriously. When's the last time we could comfortably and confidently say that about two journalists on opposing sides and the way they engage with the ideals of their day?

Now, unfortunately and with trepidation, we have to turn our eyes to the modern day. Where do we even begin to discuss, among all the institutions breaking down, the institution that was home to both Kempton and Buckley, that of journalism?

The sense-making apparatuses of our culture have, quite simply, stopped making sense. The ACLU (we'll get there), academia, you name it.

Noted conservative columnist and Hitchensesque rabble-rouser Douglas Murray knows this well.

Not incidentally, he has written of Buckley as a "veritable magician" and his "whole life's work is a reminder that one can—and should—engage with the American public in a serious and elevated way."[31]

In that spirit of engaging with ideas in a serious way (or at least attempting to), there was a celebrated Munk debate hosted in Canada in 2022 held on the question of public trust in the media. The resolution: "Be it resolved, don't trust the mainstream media."[31]

Now, this may be an instance of if you have to ask the question, you may already know the answer.

Douglas Murray and former *Rolling Stone* columnist Matt Taibbi were matched against woefully overrated author Malcolm Gladwell and columnist Michelle Goldberg.

The debate could comprise its own book, let alone its own chapter. But the arguments levied by Murray and Taibbi equated to the single largest margin of victory in the history of the debates. So, that seems a decent pulpit from which to preach.

Matt Taibbi, who might be known to some readers as the man who helped Elon Musk leak the Twitter files, kicked off the festivities by pointing out how the venerated Walter Cronkite was twice voted the most trusted person in America.

That it is all but impossible in today's society to honestly expect a journalist anywhere to take up that mantle was, in effect, the problem. He further pointed out, correctly in my view, that trust in media would be impossible to conjure again given our tribal environment.

As if to mirror the general contempt and smugness the mainstream media seem to have—and this is incidentally more than slightly indicative of an institution that has become ideologically captured—Gladwell rather nastily implied Taibbi was racist for pining for days "dominated by white men."[31] Once again, it wasn't even an attempt at understanding Taibbi's argument, much less a good effort. Taibbi called it a lunatic reaction to an offhand comment. This was a toxic compound of what debaters will recognize as the fallacy known as straw manning with an f ad hom touch.

Those twin impulses of intellectual dishonesty and lack of curiosity are also culturally offensive acts that should be examined from all sides. There is some rather sinister tribal machinery backing those impulses as well.

Murray approached the pulpit and went on a fulminating tirade of specific instances when the tribal media had indeed done their jobs out of bias, and that bias impacted their reporting and thus earned the risible responses they received from society at large.

Murray began by running roughshod over one partial bastion of supposedly journalist integrity: *The New York Times*. He called to attention that the home of "all the news that is fit to print" implied a great number of seedy ideals about an entire country—Britain—for its decision to vote to leave the European Union. Indeed, the degrading concept of tribalism is, sadly, available for immediate export abroad.

Since 2016, Murray noted, there has been a noticeable absence of positive coverage about Britain in *The New York Times.* He listed examples, including a scathing "culinary review" depicting traditional British cuisine as centered around "mutton and oatmeal." He also referenced an anti-Brexit piece from a writer in Lancaster, a city in the north of England, who was forced to acknowledge that nearly all his factual claims were wrong though, he still insisted, his "perception was correct." In this, Murray highlighted a form of smugness and lack of accountability that has increasingly become evident, at the very least perceptually, in journalism today.

I hold no particular brief for the dearly departed Queen of England, nor do I hold any great love of the monarchy in general, but Murray further revealed to the great shame that the *NYT* will not be capable of feeling:

> When her majesty the Queen died, not ten days of mourning was observed at *The New York Times*, three hours before they started attacking the Queen, and they did so day after day after day because they hate Brexit Britain. That is just an agenda! That is not anything else.[32]

He called to attention the much-maligned wave of truckers' protests in Ottawa, the well-named Freedom Convoy that occurred in Canada in early 2022. It started with a convoy of truckers who journeyed from different regions of Canada to Ottawa, the capital, to oppose COVID-19 vaccine mandates and other public health restrictions enforced by the Canadian government.

Now, the job of a reporter, as Murray pointed out though he shouldn't need to, is to report. To ask questions. To try, with the hopefully refined skill of curiosity, to get at the truth. Canada was having none of that. In the state-owned media (in most cases it pays to give a slanted eye toward anything that is state-owned) the prime minister decided, as Murray put it, "these people were . . . Nazis, they were white supremacists, they were antisemites, they were probably homophobes, they were misogynists, they are probably transphobes."[32]

This is a particular societal ill that has reached the terminal stages as "he did all the things you do in the modern political age if you just want to defenestrate someone who is awkward to you."[32] One can almost feel Buckley grimacing from the great beyond.

Douglas Murray addressed the issue with characteristic bluntness, focusing on the relationship between the Canadian government and its media: "Now, at such a time, what would the mainstream media do? It would question it. It would question it. The Canadian mainstream media did not. The Canadian mainstream media acted as an arm and chorus of the Canadian government."

Murray continued with several pointed examples: "You had a CBC host describing the Freedom Convoy as a, quote, 'feral mob.' You had a *Toronto Star* columnist saying, quote—sorry for the language—it's a 'homegrown hate farm that was then jet-fueled by an American right-funded rat-f***ing operation.' Jesus, they cannot even write at these papers anymore."[32]

Murray highlighted further cases of selective reporting:

> CBC said that two Indigenous women were so scared to go outside in Ottawa because of racist violence. Did not bother to mention that Indigenous drummers had led the truckers in an "O Canada" rendition. The *National Observer* said that the many Black and Indigenous Freedom

> Convoy supporters were, in fact, duped by the truckers. *The Globe and Mail* reporter said, "My 13-year-old son told me to tell protesters I'm not a Jew, " out of fear of anti-Semitic violence, without mentioning that one of the leaders of the convoy was himself Jewish.

He then went on to explain why he viewed the media's role as deeply compromised:

> Now, why is this so rancid—utterly, utterly rancid and corrupt? Because in this country, [Canada's] media, [Canada's] mainstream media, is funded by the government—a totally corrupted system. In 2018—oh, election year, coincidence?—the Canadian media was given $595 million over five years. The *Toronto Star* estimated it was going to be getting $3 million from the government in the first half of the year. It went on and on.

Murray tied the media's acquiescence to larger concerns about government overreach:

> So you see, the government in Canada can tell people to—they can tell the banks to shut down people's bank accounts. Oh yeah, your government can do that. And if you're happy with that, just think about what would happen if the shoe was on the other foot. The government can do that. But in Canada, they can also tell the media what to do, and the media does the bidding of the Canadian government. That isn't a free society's media. I've seen unfree countries all my life, but this in a developed liberal democracy like Canada is a disgrace.[32]

Now, yes, let's make the necessary propitiation: it was, Canada, a country, like most countries, does not enjoy the spoils of having something as glorious as the First Amendment enshrined in its founding documents.

Nonetheless, even without such constitutional protections, the media in any country bears or at least should bear the responsibility of holding power to account. Believe it or not, the Good Book has a word or two to say about this obligation. Proverbs 31:8–9 reminds us:

> Open your mouth for the mute,
> for the rights of all who are destitute.
> Open your mouth, judge righteously,
> defend the rights of the poor and needy. [Bible - 11]

Seems a decent dictum for any institution concerned with representing the interests of their people.

To see it happily relinquish that duty, especially in a time of governmental overreach, signals a deeper failure of the institutions meant to safeguard public discourse. When a nation's media becomes indistinguishable from its government, the essential checks on authority begin to erode. And it is in those moments—when the press fails to ask the difficult questions—the freedoms of the people, and the integrity of democratic society, are most at risk.

Douglas's intellectual escapades, not irrelevantly, led to a remarkable shift in voter sentiment, with support swinging from 48-52 percent against to 67-33 percent in favor—a 39 percent change, the largest in the event's history.

But, alas, Murray's recounting is far from an exhaustive list, all of which were subject to the great distortions and misrepresentations sadly becoming so common among the mainstream media.

There are some more salient examples of not only the media's dishonesty in its appeal to tribalism but also representative of the side of the aisle the media seems to call home.

A comprehensive collection of all the yet-to-be-acknowledged-let-alone-apologized-for dishonesty of the media would comprise its own voluminous set of books.

But one instance which seems to, like the snows of yesteryear, melted out of our memory was the instructive case of Bubba Smith.

It was around the middle of 2020 at, arguably, one of the heights of racial tension in our country given George Floyd and the "mostly peaceful" protests we were all treated to in its aftermath. It was reported—and the mainstream media happily proliferated the stories without troubling themselves with verifying—NASCAR driver Bubba Wallace, the only black driver in NASCAR, was the victim of a hate crime.

The hate crime in question? A rope tied to a garage door at the Talladega Speedway in Florida, supposedly in the shape of a noose.

The story was jumped on by the bloodthirsty media, who descended in a piranha-like frenzy not to that speedway to ask questions—which is after all (along with an eye and impulse toward skepticism) the job of journalists—but to retreat to their ideologically-fortified tribes for a mass exodus to spin alley. Not an alley one expects Kempton or Buckley would have walked down.

It was investigated, which I have no quarrel with, but the media was already reporting on it as if it were the established first step in a modern-day lynching. Not so.

The FBI concluded Wallace was not targeted by a hate crime and the noose had been hanging on the garage door since October 2019. It was, effectively, a hoax. One propped up and promulgated by the media.

"The FBI report concludes, and photographic evidence confirms, that the garage door pull rope fashioned like a noose had been positioned there since as early as last fall," NASCAR said in its own statement. "This was obviously well before the 43 team's arrival and garage assignment."[33]

"We appreciate the FBI's quick and thorough investigation and are thankful to learn that *this was not an intentional, racist act against Bubba*. We remain steadfast in our commitment to providing a welcoming and inclusive environment for all who love racing."[33]

This was a fairly clear-cut case of the media not doing its job in reporting the facts and asking questions. Questions like "Has this rope always been there?"

But lies of omission—leaving the areas of darkness needing to be illuminated by journalism instead dimmed further by journalism—can be just as harmful.

Is hiding a truth worse than propagating a lie?

On the matter of illumination, one must make a momentary bow in the direction of Emile Zola, rightfully thought of as one of the founders of the great profession of reportage. As part of his research for what would become *Germinal*, he spent some time down in the coal mine near the Belgian border. When he was down in the pit, he found there were enormous horses in the dark tunnels dragging the coal to and fro. Zola was quite taken aback by this and remarked to the coal miners, "These are amazingly big horses. How do you get them down here?" They laughed at him and said, "Monsieur Zola, you have much to learn. These horses are born down here. They never see the light."

Sadly, there are far too many individuals—and they seem to prefer journalism as a career—who will content themselves with the darkness surrounding them. When the truth is kept in darkness, with no sunlight, that is how the shadow of untruth or—to resort to a popular term—misinformation prevails.

So, it was late June in 2024 when then-President Joe Biden debated then-former President Donald Trump at Techwood Turner campus in Atlanta, Georgia.

In summary, the debate was the strictest definition of "catastrophic" for Biden. On display before millions of Americans was a man who simply did not know where or perhaps even who he was.

I don't mean to make a cynical point or score an ideological jab here. It was genuinely sad to see.

He floundered, he stumbled, and it was punctuated with one of the main memes exported from the fiasco: "We beat Medicare." The height of cognitive decline was showcased for, quite literally, the world to see.

In fact, Biden's performance wasn't terribly surprising for many Americans, perhaps even a solid half.

A steady diet of the former Senator's fumbles, stumbles, and mumbles was constantly fed to the American people, more or less, whenever Biden spoke. You know the rest of *that* story already, dear reader. Amidst mass outrage and pressure, Biden was more or less forced to announce he wouldn't seek re-election, clearing the ground for Vice President Kamala Harris to have her shot at rising to the highest political office in America.

But the great wickedness perpetrated by the media writ large was, once again, a shocking outcome of hypertribalism.

There seemed to be a conspiracy—yes, I said it: conspiracy—by the media to keep Biden's clear cognitive decline safely off the table of general cultural discussion.

Don't take my word for it.

We can simply look to that bastion of neutrality *The Wall Street Journal*, finally, for some true illumination.

National Review, in a piece aptly titled "WSJ: The Conspiracy to Hide Biden's Condition Is Nearly Three

Years Old," recalls how the good journal was able to put a date on the "start of the cover-up of Biden's senility."

The *WSJ* recounted when "President Biden had just finished trying to persuade a group of congressional Democrats to pass a $1 trillion infrastructure bill when Nancy Pelosi, then the House speaker, took the microphone." According to Democrats present, the piece revealed, Biden spoke in a disjointed manner during his thirty minutes of remarks on Capitol Hill without making a clear request of the lawmakers.

After Biden departed, the obviously frustrated Speaker of the House Nancy Pelosi told the group she would clarify what he had been attempting to convey in an effort to make sense out of nonsense, one lawmaker reported.

"It was the first time I remember people pretty jarred by what they had seen," recalled Rep. Dean Phillips (D-Minn.), who would go on to mount an unsuccessful primary challenge against the president.

It was clearly a sign of things to come.

That was October 2021, the *WSJ* bleakly clarified. That month was the last time Biden met with the House Democratic Caucus on the Hill regarding legislation. This was over three years before Biden shuffled himself onto that debate stage in Georgia.[100]

Later, in 2022, according to the Daily Beast, came a slightly less serious but nonetheless blindingly illuminating display. In September 2022, at a hunger conference, President Joe Biden looked out at the audience and asked, "Jackie, are you here? Where's Jackie?" Silence followed. "I think she was… she was going to be here," he added.

Jackie Walorski, who was one of the conference organizers, had tragically died in a car accident the month prior.

The White House expressed condolences on Biden's behalf after her death, acknowledging how he "appreciated her partnership" in organizing the event. White House Press Secretary Karine Jean-Pierre later explained Biden's inquiry by saying Walorski was "top of mind" for him at the conference—a phrase she repeated over a dozen times when reporters pressed her. But this answer made little sense: if Walorski had truly been "top of mind" for Biden, then her passing would have been as well.[101]

Perhaps it's no wonder then, according to presidential scholar Martha Kumar's analysis, Axios reported in July 2024, Biden held fewer press conferences and media interviews at that stage in his term than any of the previous seven presidents—a decision or "strategy," by the way, demanding its own line of inquiry.[102]

One person who might well agree with my characterization of the media's thunderous silence on Biden's mental state, interestingly enough, would be Democratic Representative Lloyd Doggett who, in the immediate aftermath of the 2024 debate—what Biden would call a "bad episode"—called it out in an interview he did for *Journal*, which also acted as a call for Biden to drop out of the 2024 race.

"I am really concerned about what we were not told during these months," said Rep. Lloyd Doggett (D-Tex.) in an interview. "I remain concerned about that—that for whatever reasons, this overprotective, stage-managed kind of operation not only appears to have denied the American people broadly of an understanding of the president's current situation, but also other elected officials."

So, while I'll grant he didn't use the word *conspiracy*, he didn't exactly *not* call it such.

So, what was the media's role in this cover-up? It was its en masse commitment to staying loyal to their liberal tribes and preventing the sparks of curiosity from igniting in service to getting to the truth of Biden.

A fairly simple thought experiment, dear reader, is to suppose it was Donald Trump, as president, who instead botched a pitch to his own party while trying to pass a significant infrastructure bill. Would that spark evolve into a media firestorm?

As ideologically partisan as that may sound, it actually isn't. We all, left or right, have a concern—whether or not we admit the concern when asked—that our media, as we often say, speaking truth to power and holding that power to account.

But, alas, such a lack of curiosity, amounting to complicity, is one of the plethora of consequences on offer to a culture embracing tribalism and the demonization of the other side. That demonization bleeds through to actions of the institutions we had, at least at one point, held dear. Journalism is one of those casualties that needs extensive social operations to be made well again.

For his part, Buckley was once asked by a CSPAN caller as early as 2000 about the "increasingly liberal" tendencies of the mainstream media (with CNN called out in particular) to add their own "slant" on the news and to simply "ignoring stories" (such as the Biden debacle that would show up over two decades later): the called asked if he noticed the tendency and what he might think about it.

"I think that it's one of the forces of nature that we have to contend with. The critical community gets its life and its inspiration from the temptation to criticize," Buckley answered. "There was a poll published two or three years ago that said that between 75 and 80% percent of the people engaged in television journalism had voted Democratic in the previous election."

"When I was at Yale," Buckley went on, "a professor to whom I was very attached disclosed a poll taken of tenured professors in the department of political science. There were 23 of them." The question on offer to them was "Dewey or Truman?" "23 Truman; Dewey none," Buckley revealed.[98] This was about the presidential election of 1948 between Thomas Dewey and Harry S. Truman.

These examples are, sadly and—even more depressingly—obviously, an unfinished picture of the stratospheric levels of dishonesty and partisanship so virulently present in the media and journalism in our day. But if the point hasn't been made by now that the mainstream media has been perhaps irreversibly poisoned by tribalism, then I don't think the point is likely to hit you regardless of whose words you read.

CHAPTER 6

Allard Lowenstein: Crossing Political Boundaries

If one has to wonder what sort of politician Buckley would have made, one would not need wonder long. The supreme ruler of *National Review* made his views and positions known not only in print and on *Firing Line*, but of course during his campaign for the mayoral nomination in New York City in 1965.

As it was, Mr. Buckley's older brother, James, was a New York senator and later a judge, courtesy of the nomination of family friend and longtime *NR* subscriber Ronald Reagan.

During his 1970 campaign, Buckley, the columnist, wrote to Reagan asking for a letter of support for his would-be senator brother. Reagan happily obliged but, alas, James was defeated by opponent Daniel P. Moynihan, 54.1 to 44.1 percent.

Buckley took a back seat in his brother's second go at the Senate in 1976, but here it was a public stance WFB took on another New York race that irked many of his fellow conservatives.

That Buckley turned out to publicly support in print in *National Review* the liberal activist Allard Lowenstein's doomed run for the fifth congressional district in 1976—rather than toe the party line with an endorsement of the Republican incumbent John Wydler might be the best answer to anyone who would accuse Buckley of simply being a right-wing idealogue.

In 2000, in a televised discussion with Brian Lamb, a caller asked Buckley his thoughts on Lowenstein.

"I knew him when he was at law school at Yale and I was teaching Spanish," Buckley revealed.

But Buckley went on to say, "I didn't really get to experience him until 1968 when, in the Chicago convention [this was the Democratic National Congress to which he was a delegate] he, in my judgment, behaved with considerable maturity. He was running for Congress, in fact, he was elected, and he was so appealing, so bright, such a good sport, such a marvelous sense of humor that I ended up actually urging his election."

He had but one response to people who couldn't understand why he would engage in, as he put it, "such an act of heterodoxy."

"Self-indulgence," he rather cryptically answered. "I had no other excuse for it."[98]

Lowenstein was first thrust into the national spotlight back in 1968 when, as a chief architect of the "Dump Johnson Movement," he aided Minnesota Democrat Senator Eugene McCarthy in undermining LBJ's campaign for the presidency. It was primarily an interparty schism separating antiwar liberals (of which Lowenstein was a salient figure) and moderates, among others.

Senator James Buckley found himself having to respond after his brother's column stirred up not only

Representative John W. Wydler, Al Lowenstein's Republican opponent, but also Assemblyman Joseph M. Margiotta, the influential Nassau County Republican leader. Margiotta's discontent was particularly concerning because his backing was crucial to Buckley's re-election campaign.

In an effort to smooth things over, Senator Buckley stepped away from his own campaign to publicly support Wydler. While his endorsement wasn't as eloquent as his brother's writings, it was equally generous.

He praised Wydler, saying he "has demonstrated since his election in 1962 that integrity and leadership and concern for the taxpayer and the wage earner—qualities not always evident in Congress—can be brought to bear on problems confronting the American people."

A rather powerful wave of political consternation washed over Conservative party officials, and those sea levels must have risen higher still when Buckley once again supported Lowenstein two years later (following his loss in 1976), albeit in a different district.

In that column, Buckley praised Lowenstein further, "who was once the head of Americans for Democratic Action and bears those disfiguring scars with fortitude," scars suffered for the Democrat's position on the right of nonpublic schools to receive their share of state aid.[99]

"This is the first time he supported me for any office, and I'm very grateful," Mr. Lowenstein said of William Buckley's endorsement in an interview. "We've grown over the years to respect each other's viewpoints, and I'm fond of Bill Buckley as a human being."

"This is only the beginning of what will develop during the campaign into a broad-based Republican-Conservative support for my candidacy," Mr. Lowenstein said. "There will be other major figures who will endorse me who have been prominent Conservatives and Republicans."

Buckley, the now-former senator, playfully rebuked his brother for supporting Mr. Lowenstein, humorously referring to him as "puckish" on multiple occasions.

With a smile, the senator remarked, "I can now reveal a closely held family secret. Brother Bill associates with me, and he's even befriended some rather charming, though undeniably liberal, figures like Allard Lowenstein."

In my conversation with *National Review's* Rich Lowry, he reflected on Buckley's surprising endorsement of Lowenstein.

"For Bill, personal relationships were more important than the political," Lowry noted. Buckley was a strong believer in conviction and sincerity. "If he felt convinced that you were a left-winger who believed for the right reasons, held it sincerely, and could argue for it, he'd have respect for you, even to the extent of endorsing someone like Al Lowenstein, which seems a little crazy to me," Lowry said.

This insight underscores a key aspect of Buckley's character: despite his staunch conservatism, he valued personal relationships over political differences. As the current editor-in-chief of *National Review* summed up, "He put relationships over politics."

And *that* should be the rallying cry for all Americans in our unforgivably tribal society.

Lowenstein made nine separate appearances on *Firing Line* with the last one, in early 1980, being only ninety days before his untimely death.

It was May that same year when the antiwar activist met his demise when he was shot by former political protégé and friend Dennis Sweeney. Sweeney, who suffered from paranoid schizophrenia, believed Lowenstein was part of a conspiracy against him. Lowenstein, in true form, had tried to help Sweeney in the past with his mental health issues, but their relationship deteriorated as Sweeney's paranoia worsened.

Buckley gave a eulogy at the memorial service for Lowenstein three days after the tragedy in New York City.

In a heartfelt speech, Buckley warmly praised Lowenstein's strength of character, saying the New Jersey native was "at home with collectivist formulations," and "one had the impression that he might be late in aborting a third world war because of his absorption with the problems of one sophomore."

"Of all the artisans I have known, from the furthest steps of the spectrum, his was the most undistracted concern not for humanity—though he was conversant with big-think idiom—but for human beings."[90]

This important point of Lowenstein not just caring for people in that abstract, nebulous sense so familiar to activists starved for a kind of cosmic justice but on the microlevel, on an individual basis, should not be overlooked.

Buckley described him as the "original activist" of our times.

Senator Bobby Kennedy noted at the funeral the great breadth of friendships Lowenstein held, as evident in the audience as it was among the speakers. "Who but Al could have as friends Bill Buckley and Bobby Kennedy?" he asked.[89] Buckley would loathe the use of the term, but it could be said the two were "fellow travelers" in the sense that both men observed a commitment to build bridges, not burn them. Friendship can transcend political differences, which perhaps should be irrelevant, or in fact fuel the glorious hunt for rewarding friendships.

Buckley's respect for Lowenstein reached such magnificent heights he dedicated an entire episode to him and his political adventures in "Allard Lowenstein on *Firing Line:* A Retrospective."

At the risk of belaboring a point, this was a Republican's treatment of supposedly, at least on its face, a political adversary. Those earlier endorsements, much to the chagrin of the Right which did indeed include his own senator brother, would comprise those tensions between party loyalty and personal principles.

The Catholic icon didn't mind shirking his conservative brethren and supporting Lowenstein when it made sense to him. A slight rephrase of this might be Buckley told the truth in his heart. And when one tells the unmitigated truth, it means one does not quite know what road his words will lead him down. And *that* means they get to go on an adventure.

Adventure.

A terribly important endeavor to which we might return in modern society. It seems the ideal of adventure is yet another casualty of the tribal nature in which we live.

One wonders if that sense of adventure Buckley displayed throughout his life—let's not forget he sailed across the Atlantic twice (once with J. K. Galbraith); he sailed across the Pacific once; he worked in the CIA (under then-future Watergate acolyte Howard Hunt); and he served in the Army—isn't linked to his Christian ethic as well.

Taking his son Christopher's word, which I would be heavily inclined to for obvious reasons, if his faith was indeed the "molten core" of him, then it would have to be linked by definition.

One of my favorite definitions of God I have thus far heard was one thrown into the public space by Dr. Jordan Peterson when he was in conversation with Hitchens-adjacent atheist Sam Harris.

Peterson defined God as, among other things, "that eternal call to adventure."[72]

Adventure, in this sense, is more than just ephemeral thrill-seeking. It's both the bold pursuit of truth, central to the Christian ethic, as Buckley would have pointed out, and the willingness to step beyond comfort, to explore, and to grow. Buckley's journey—whether through debates, transideological friendships, or political risk—was, at its heart, an adventure oriented toward understanding, having difficult discussions, and seeking truth regardless the ideological damage it might inflict. In other words, pursuing truth to its furthest end.

"Each of you must put off falsehood and speak truthfully to your neighbor, for we are all members of one body," Ephesians 4:25 heartily adds. [Bible - 12]

Was Buckley summoning the adventurous spirit within him in supporting Lowenstein? We are slaves to speculation in most ways on this point, but I think the most sensible answer is a stout and hearty *yes.*

To return to the modern context, what could possibly be less adventurous than battening down the hatches of our respective echo chambers and sequestering with our tribe, safe from the potentially penetrating ideals and opinions of those with whom we disagree?

If we classify such ideological fastening as unadventurous, then surely its pole—the venturing out into the wilderness of ideals with the common obstacles of debate, confrontation, and the pursuit of truth (or our closest approximation of it) at all costs—is the epitome of adventure seeking.

The three transcendent values Plato famously argued, are truth, beauty, and goodness. These traits also play off each other. In other words, if something is true, it has a higher likelihood of being good and thus beautiful, at least on the level of ordinary, perhaps divinely permitted intuitions.

Buckley might advise us to consider, in our best efforts to ward off the intellectual atrophy and routine of non-adventure, since God is the source of all existence and the sole necessary being, He can (perhaps only) be understood through the lens of these transcendent qualities. While His creations possess goodness, truth, and beauty in a relative sense, only God embodies them in their fullest, absolute form. Therefore, while creatures may be described as "good," "true," and "beautiful," only God is Goodness, Truth, and Beauty.

I fully admit I am slightly throwing words directly down the gullet of Mr. Buckley, but I daresay he would perish the thought of arguing against the idea that God is good. God is true. And, above all, God is beautiful.

So, the grand adventure of maximizing psychological and social well-being in our culture might be to take a long deep inhalation and breathe a sense of truth, beauty, and goodness into the morally dormant American body via a steady treatment of a return to truthful speech, which is the highest Christian ethic by its own definition.

An obsession with the truth, as we all should have, can no question have its disadvantages particularly in today's culture where the dictates of the tribe reign supreme and will so often run counter to the truth.

But Buckley was obsessed with the truth. Only such a man would pen the ominously titled and undoubtedly chagrin-inducing *National Review* piece "It Didn't Work."

It was the bombing of a Shiite mosque in Samara that prompted the piece and induced Buckley to write the starling admission confessing, "ours is a failed mission."

The broader application of the article was an admonishment to those on the Right (at least primarily) for falling for the second Bush administration's campaign in Iraq.

The dark road of support for the incursion into Iraq seemed to curl into a question mark for Buckley, and it was a question he wanted to try to resolve.

"What Mr. Bush proposes to do," Buckley wrote, "is to unseat Saddam Hussein and to eliminate his investments in aggressive weaponry. We can devoutly hope that internecine tribal antagonisms will be subsumed in the fresh air of a despot removed, and that the restoration of freedom will be productive."

"But," Buckley wrote on, "these concomitant developments can't be either foreseen by the United States or implemented by us. What Mr. Bush can accomplish is the removal of a regime and its infrastructure. The Iraqi people will have to take it from there."[73]

That is an enviable commitment to the truth from the man whom many who should know better would out-of-hand condemn on the charge of being an idealogue.

As it stands now, we live in a decidedly unadventurous culture largely unconcerned with the truth, so long as it toes the party line and denigrates the opposing tribe.

When those on the Left who should—and, worse, perhaps even *do*—know better try to convict Trump and, to a large extent, Trump supporters on the ridiculous charge of Nazism or Nazi sympathy, they never seem more bright-eyed and bushy-tailed than when bringing up the long debunked myth that Trump said there were good people on both sides of the infamous Charlottesville rally.

They will try to pin him down on the idea that he called neo-Nazis and white Supremacists "good people." They care not at all for the pit of exculpation Trump immediately climbed out of when he said, *in the same speech* in August 2017, he wasn't "talking about the neo-Nazis and the white nationalists because *they should be condemned totally*."[74]

It was, in fact, this lie which compelled Biden to seek the presidency.

"When the president was asked what he thought had happened, Donald Trump said—and I quote—'There are very fine people on both sides.' My God, that's what he said. That is what he said and what he meant," Biden said during his speech.

"That's when I realized—had to listen to the admonition of my dead son—I could not stay on the sidelines. So, I ran."[75]

Legendary Democratic activist and strategist James Carville, who either didn't know but more than likely didn't care, went on *Real Time with Bill Maher* as late as December 2023 and spouted the obvious lie.

This is willful and proud ignorance of the truth, coupled with a torrent of bad faith they will readily douse on anyone sympathetic to the Right and modern conservatism.

This selective hearing and distortion of Trump's words reflect a broader trend among those who dismiss or deliberately mischaracterize the modern conservative movement. But this tactic is not new. Buckley faced countless attacks and misrepresentations throughout his career, particularly when leading efforts to refine and legitimize conservatism in the public eye. One might instance an infamous moment where eternal liberal Gore Vidal called Buckley a "crypto-nazi."

Buckley's ability to navigate these ideological battles, while fostering an intellectual safe space (I can be ironic too) for truth-seeking voices, set a precedent that reverberated through future conservative institutions.

A prime example of this is the way Buckley quietly inspired key figures who would go on to shape the future of conservative thought in unexpected ways. His influence, often subtle and behind the scenes, set in motion a ripple effect reaching far beyond his own public battles, giving rise to voices and movements that continue to challenge the status quo today.

Buckley, in a sort of cultural instance of Adam Smith's "invisible hand," helped others on their own adventure to find their voice of truth as he endeavored to find his own.

One could easily reference the case of Professor Jeffrey Hart and his founding of the conservative—yes, conservative—college newspaper *The Dartmouth Review.*

Jeffrey Hart, former Navy man and English literature PhD from Columbia, joined *National Review* in 1962 as a book reviewer and would later become a senior editor. It was Hart who would go on to play a crucial role not only in *National Review* but also in opening the curtain on his own adventure.

He would, soon enough, begin making the almost five-hour trip from Hanover, New Hampshire, to New York every other week to assist with the editorial section, and he proved himself invaluable to the operation running as smoothly as it did. When Buckley and Burnham were out on any number of the various appointments beckoning them, it was Hart who manned the helm of the editorial section.

Every other Tuesday, the blue-eyed professor would make the trip to New York from Hanover, arriving with unusual punctuality at the offices of *National Review* for the editorial conference.

NR Managing Editor Priscilla Buckley fondly recalled Hart as a "man of deep learning and wide interests" who could be entrusted to pen an educated and lyrical editorial on "anything from football to Maria Callas." She went on to christen Hart as "the perfect colleague"[25] who was the ideal figure to have by one's side, particularly in times of turmoil when the skill of crisis management becomes particularly useful.

In a picture of academia that mimics, perhaps in its embryonic form, the situation we find ourselves in today, Professor Hart stood out as the conservative oasis amidst the prevailing desert of liberal sentiments generally found within the Dartmouth faculty in the late 1960s and 1970s.The man was a beacon for many young men and women who would first attend his much-discussed and celebrated lectures, who would then be drawn in by his ideals and willingness to engage with them.

It was this collection of like-minded Dartmouth constituents who would found the humble but bold college journal *The Dartmouth Review*. The *Review's* escapades would sometimes earn them column inches within the pages of *The New York Times*, albeit as the subject of the critical eye from them. Mirroring the plight of the then-newly formed *National Review*, the *Times* wrote there was indeed a need for a conservative paper within the liberal confines of America's college campuses, but one had to do better than *The Dartmouth Review*.

Ripple effects abound because it was as an editor at *The Dartmouth Review* a bright-eyed Dartmouth student named Dinesh D'Souza caught the talent-scouting eye of Professor Hart. D'Souza, after then getting conscripted to write a series of pieces for *National Review*, later served as a policy adviser for Reagan and wrote his own screed against liberalism's proliferation on college campuses in 1991, *Illiberal Education*. D'Souza, still in the midst of his own adventure, haunts public political discourse to this day.

Additionally, it was at Hart's urging that *NR* hired as its editorial assistant a Dartmouth student named Peter Robinson who would go on his own adventure to become a speechwriter for Ronald Reagan. Robinson became part of the great dramas of history after he penned, for Reagan, the now-famous line "Mr. Gorbachev, tear down this wall" used in a certain June 1987 speech. Robinson continues to write for *National Review* to this day, at least at the time of this writing.

Yet another prominent name emergent from the pages of *The Dartmouth Review* and Professor Hart tutelage is that of author and political commentator Paul Gigot.

Gigot also served as an editorial assistant at the offices of *National Review* for two years following his graduation from Dartmouth.

From there, Gigot, on the dime of a Luce journalistic fellowship, picked up work and study in the Far East. While there, he was seen and scooped up by *The Wall Street Journal*, where he would spend the next fourteen years writing his column "Potomac Watch." That column would eventually win Gigot the Pulitzer Prize in 2000. So, it was an adventure that certainly bore fruit for him.

This legacy of adventure seeking Buckley imparted is not merely a historical footnote.

It revealed the profound impact of pursuing the truth that lies within one's heart, seeking out the all-consuming call to adventure and inspiring others to do likewise.

Consider those paths forged by Hart and his protégés as well as how their journeys reflect the essential struggle for truth in a society often beset by confusion and moral ambiguity. Once again, the struggle for and the pursuit of truth is the highest form of adventure one can take part in.

It also is a moral imperative for those who wish to climb out of the sludge of anti-intellectual tribalism we find ourselves in currently. Buckley's belief in the importance of a strong moral compass is more relevant today than ever, urging us to reflect on the principles shaping our discourse and guiding our actions.

As Buckley might advise, we stand at a cultural crossroads, and a reorientation toward God in our culture would correct this lack of concern for the Truth facing us daily in our political, social, and moral spheres. Failing that and failing to answer that morally mandated call to adventure, America will simply become a moral ghost ship listlessly drifting through a sea of moral relativism and bad faith, in both theological and rhetorical senses.

CHAPTER 7

Arthur Schlesinger Jr.: Respectful Adversaries

It may be odd for a critic and polemicist to say that he or she may have the capacity and indeed streak of friendliness within them. Public and litigious disputes with the likes of Gore Vidal aside, Buckley in many ways exemplified having political *opponents,* but not political *enemies.* A salient case here would be his fair-minded and respectful, but nonetheless charged and energetic relationship with Arthur Schlesinger Jr.. Buckley clearly had quite a degree of respect for the famed Kennedy historian.

He was a close adviser to John F. Kennedy and later the author of *A Thousand Days: John F. Kennedy in the White House,* which earned him a Pulitzer Prize, one of two he achieved in his lifetime.

Buckley at least twice referenced Schlesinger in debate. The first was with Gore Vidal on ABC when he invoked his name to sharpen a point he was making that Vidal would renounce his American citizenship if Nixon won. The second was during a *Firing Line* debate with New Left darling Noam Chomsky. Buckley invoked the name of left-leaning Schlesinger when referring to Professor Chomsky's "own intolerance of other people's point of view."

Schlesinger, for his part, wrote often of his admiration for Buckley's rhetorical skills, as well as his wit. He remarked on Buckley's ability to take "readers on a lively and tempestuous journey." Commenting on Buckley's book *McCarthy and His Enemies*, coauthored with his brother-in-law L. Brent Bozell (himself the ghostwriter of the 1960's *The Conscience of a Conservative*) referred to the book admirably, with perhaps a tinge of jealousy, as a "clever and sick" literary work.[76]

Friendly comments aside, it must not be forgotten Buckley and Schlesinger were indeed opponents. In 1961, immediately after Kennedy—whom few venerated more than Schlesinger—became president, the two met at Newton College in Massachusetts to discuss the oft-mentioned and seldom understood welfare state.

Indeed, the first Schlesinger-centered sentence to spill out of Buckley's pen onto the pages of *National Review* was in April 1958, when Buckley wrote—let's not forget he did have a polemical spirit within him—that Arthur's "obsessive partisanship has disqualified him as a historian."[50]

Not exactly a friendship-fomenting line.

The two met, only just after Kennedy took office, to debate at Newton College of the Sacred Heart in Massachusetts over the benefits—or lack thereof—of the welfare state.

Buckley, anticipating the audience would be evenly divided, remarked how Schlesinger was more familiar with speaking in environments "where they preach academic freedom and practice liberal indoctrination." He also criticized Schlesinger's behavior, which Buckley later described as "oleaginous." Schlesinger, in turn, opened his remarks with a sarcastic comment, saying Buckley had "a facility for rhetoric, which I envy, as well as a wit which I seek clumsily to emulate."[92]

Later, Buckley reprinted Schlesinger's comment in *Rumbles Left and Right: A Book About Troublesome People and Ideas*, using it as a blurb without Schlesinger's permission. When Schlesinger threatened legal action, Buckley responded by asserting the quote was part of the public record. After Schlesinger complained to Buckley's publisher, Buckley humorously replied, "Tell Arthur . . . not to take it so hard: No one believes a thing he says anyway."[93]

He even copied Schlesinger on the letter and signed it with the return address reading, "Wm. Envy His Rhetoric Buckley." In his letter to Schlesinger's attorneys, Buckley wrote, "Now, there is a very good case to be made for everyone's apologizing who has ever quoted Arthur Schlesinger; but isn't it droll to be asked to apologize to Schlesinger for quoting from Schlesinger."[92]

According to James Rosen, the Kennedy historian wrote in his private diary entry in 1995—which wouldn't be seen by the public eye until six months after Buckley's death—a brief reminiscence of a joint appearance the two made on *The Charlie Rose Show*. He wrote how their appearances "must have disappointed all those who looked forward to a slam-bang, no-holds-barred fight." Schlesinger wrote following his own viewing of the program that it looked very much like "old gladiators who in their genial decline were substituting jollity for combat."[50]

In the midst of a tiff, Arthur Schlesinger Jr. wrote Buckley, referring to "*National Review* or *National Enquirer* or whatever your magazine calls itself," to which WFB answered, "Now suppose I began a letter, 'Dear Arthur or Dear Barfer or whatever you call yourself'?"[91]

Harkening back to those combative days, perhaps falling through the trapdoor of nostalgia no doubt triggering for us all, Schlesinger wrote that back when he "really disliked" Buckley, he entered himself into a *National Review* contest of some sort and, in fact, won. Buckley had his own sense of mischief.

That award, by the way, was *National Review*'s Special Award for Promise in Political Prognostication.

Marion Schlesinger, Arthur's wife of thirty years, recounts the prize to, in fact, Kitty Galbraith, wife of JKG, when the two were brought together. Their correspondence was elegantly captured by *Harvard Magazine* in 1996.

"We'd moved into this home, and one day I was taking some varnish off furniture with paint remover," explains the fairer Galbraith. "The housekeeper came to me and said, 'Mrs. Galbraith, there's a donkey in the Schlesingers' yard.' I thought, 'Oh, dear, too much paint remover.' "

But in fact there *was* a donkey, shipped as a prank to the Schlesingers by someone no doubt enjoying a belly laugh.

"I'd come back from shopping at Filene's Basement, and there was this donkey on the front lawn," Marian Schlesinger remembers.

"It came from this pain in the neck Bill Buckley. The children were sitting on its back. Arthur was off campaigning. The animal was hungry, and there was no food for it—it was eating everything in sight; we went to the neighbors to get some garden clippings to feed it. Five people tried to push it into a station wagon to take it away, but the animal would not budge. Finally, I realized that Stephen [their son] had signed for it—but he was underage. So I called Railway Express and had them come and retrieve the creature."[78]

When Buckley got his ass back, he had a donkey cart built and named the animal "Arthur."

Buckley's humor, along with his indefatigable civility (unless you were Gore Vidal, George Wallace, or some insipid Bircher), have to be reckoned as his two most undervalued traits.

A sense of humor and a just as compelling sense of mischief that will assuredly mix into an extremely potent serum to induce friendship.

Indeed, Schlesinger went on to pen in the same journal entry that he "developed a regard for Bill's wit, his passion for the harpsichord, his human decency, even his compulsion to épater the liberals." He slams the door of that entry behind him as he wrote, with admirable clarity and concision, "now we are friends—and go easy on each other."[50]

Two asides to pester you with briefly: 1) Buckley's passion for the harpsichord was so fervent, it was once inscribed at the top of at least one of his harpsichords, "*SHAME on anyone who plays me badly.*"

2) Épater means "to startle or shock out of complacency." If the humble author of these words had to look up its definition, perhaps the humble reader would need to as well. Your energy can now properly be focused on reading.

Perhaps the single encapsulating summation of Buckley's and Schlesinger's relationship was made by Buckley in a charming article Buckley wrote in 2007 for *National Review* in the wake of Schlesinger's death by a heart attack. Buckley wrote, in spite of Arthur's earlier statement, "I always regretted that we didn't become friends, because the thousands who succeeded in doing so found friendship with Arthur Schlesinger very rewarding."[79]

The salient point to linger on where our current ethos is concerned would be Schlesinger's admiration for Buckley's *human decency*.

Yes, dear reader, it is possible for someone you disagree with, even on a volatile issue, to still have decency within them. It is even more possible for that existence to be noticed. In other words, the person you're disagreeing with *is* a person and not merely your foil of the moment. To think otherwise is simply an exercise in solipsism.

One name you probably did not expect to intrude into these pages is the name *Bill Maher*. The old-school leftie comedian has recounted a number of times on his *Club Random* podcast how he has met fellow liberals whose disease of being unable to see the decency in someone with opposing views reached such a terminal stage they "didn't want to breathe the same air as a Trump supporter." It has to be granted this is anecdotal with a dash of hearsay, but can any serious person truly say this isn't indicative of where we stand in vast swaths of the culture, hunkered in our respective tribes?

A parting admonishment to close out this chapter would be to uphold what Buckley considered the Christian ethic of seeing the decency which usually lurks within others. Christianity emphasizes love, compassion, and forgiveness as central virtues. Virtues even a secularist or humanist can appreciate. In the teachings of Jesus, believers are encouraged to love their neighbors as themselves (Mark 12:31) and even to love their enemies (Matthew 5:44). This ethic urges individuals to look beyond differences, faults, and conflicts and to recognize the inherent dignity and worth in every person, as all are made in the image of God (Genesis 1:27).

But these values are readily and, in fact, encouraged to be available for immediate export and emulation by those who don't subscribe to, say, the Catholic doctrine.

The point is, decency should be viewed in the same vein as courtroom innocence. We ought to assume decency in each other until it's proven beyond a reasonable doubt they aren't. Buckley understood this, hence his aforementioned split with Bircher Revilo Oliver. That split, incidentally, could well comprise its own book.

But when it comes to decency, modern-day conservatives and MAGA (if you insist on the term) have plenty of firm purposes of amendment and apologies to make as well. Whatever conclusion one feels inclined to come to regarding January 6—whether you think it was a genuine true-blue insurrection attempt or you think it was just a bunch of goofballs who basically took an unofficial tour of the Capitol—I think running around letting rip such tender sweet nothings as "Hang Mike Pence!" might be less than morally advisable and certainly offensive to a similarly true-blue Christian.

One would hope there's some corner of conservative soil that is forever Buckley, but it seems certainly in the case of January 6 that the soil of America's Mother Earth is either too shallow or too eroded to sustain the kind of principled, intellectually rigorous growth Buckley championed. What remains is a scorched landscape, where decency has become a casualty of tribalism and where even the most basic norms of discourse are trampled by those who prefer spectacle over substance. Such is the great societal project of repatriation at hand.

But this is the swamp of polarization that has formed, which we as Americans have let fester and proliferate. When you live beside a swamp, no amount of fly swatters will protect you. That is how you get "Hang Mike Pence!" entering common parlance, if only for a short period.

What remains is a swamp of ignorance and tribalism.

How does one—pardon the Trumpesque rhetoric—drain this swamp? I daresay Buckley's and certainly my prescription for a healthier, more decent culture is to return to times of civility and kindness where we could, in fact, disagree about politics and the like. Keep the powder of one's civility in a permanently dry state.

Better yet, there was a time not long ago when we had no idea where each other's political loyalties lay.

As Buckley said when interviewed by the incomparable Brian Lamb on C SPAN's *Summer Series*—while fielding a direct criticism put to him by *American Spectator* founder R. Emmett Tyrrell that he has too many liberal friends (a critique that should itself invite some follow-up questions)—Buckley simply stated, "I don't spend my time talking politics." There is a lesson for all of us in there, is there not?

Buckley expounded on this in the theological realm with his faith-flavored autobiography *Nearer, My God* when he wrote, clearly and boldly, "It is widely assumed… that I am a dogged evangelist of my political and economic view. It's true, but only when I write and speak publicly. Those who spend time with me know that I don't . . . ever . . . bring up my political faith unless specifically questioned about it, and this happens, among intimates, only when accidental turns of conversation lurch us onto a path that requires ideological exploration."

Speaking of Christianity and God, how about an ironic transition?

CHAPTER 8

John Kenneth Galbraith: Rivals and Friends

"I regret that."[50]

What a bizarre collection of words to kick off a decades-long friendship.

But that was, in fact, the eventual result of these words, uttered by the eternally liberal economist John Kenneth Galbraith to Buckley in the elevator of New York's Plaza Hotel in 1966. It was their first time meeting.

Not uninterestingly, if perhaps somewhat irrelevantly, the two were on their way, with their wives, to the masked Black and White Ball hosted by Truman Capote, who would publish his immortal *In Cold Blood* that same year.

But the firm purpose of amendment on offer to Buckley was regarding JKG's undertaking to warn a colleague at Harvard to not sully their good name with a byline in *National Review*.

Buckley recounts this, characterizing "Galbraith [as] The Enemy, professional and personal. Professional, because he was the standout political liberal in America; brilliant and influential teacher of teachers in the economics and politics of centralization."

One can easily see the respect, however begrudging, Buckley yielded to JKG. He did go on to explain it was "personal, because I had visited just months before a professor whose work I wanted regularly in my magazine. I learned from him that Professor Galbraith, on seeing the one article he'd written for us, wired him to say that he should ostracize *National Review*."

But that was all put to rest in that elevator, with Buckley's Christian ethic of forgiveness and grace shining through, and a lifelong friendship sprung from it. All it took was "a simple apology." That might be worth bearing in mind, dear reader.

"Two months later, in Switzerland, he invited me to ski with him," Buckley revealed.[24]

The post-Keynesian economics professor was, according to Buckley, every bit as necessary to the dismal science as Adam Smith and, indeed, Maynard Keynes.

But it was in a review WFB published of Galbraith's influential *The Culture of Contentment,* where Buckley wrote, tellingly, "'It is fortunate for Professor Galbraith that he was born with singular gifts as a writer. It is a pity he hasn't used these skills in other ways than to try year after year to bail out his sinking ships." The structure and the efficacy of these *ships*, to complete the metaphor, would comprise the central focus of most of Galbraith's eleven appearances on *Firing Line* (with the exception of the 20th anniversary special titled "Bill Buckley and *Firing Line* Get Roasted"—and no doubt JKG was especially jubilant for that taping), where they showcased every inch of their disagreements (if you have *inches* of disagreements), though one could easily spot the sugar coated barbs characterizing virtually all their utterances.

Both WFB and JKG were avid and enthusiastic skiers, both preferring the great slopes of Gstaad in Switzerland. (Buckley has even commented that he prefers skiing to writing.) Two months after that initial encounter in the New York elevator, the two met once again by chance, this time across the pond at the slopes of Switzerland.

Upon seeing Galbraith descend a slope, Buckley asked him how long he had been skiing.

"Thirty years," the almost seven-foot-tall Harvard economics professor revealed.

"That's as long as you've been studying economics," Buckley replied in a playful gibe.

Buckley recalled lovingly of his friend that he "constantly writes pleasant tributes to my own books, inevitably advising the reader that my political opinions should be ignored; my fiction or accounts of life at sea, appreciated."[24]

Perhaps the most concrete example of the particular strain of humor running virulently through their friendship comes from Galbraith's 85th birthday celebration at the Boston Public Library in October 1993, at which Buckley was a speaker.

Halfway through his four-minute speech, his talk was interrupted by that evening's master of ceremonies.

"Is there a doctor in the house?" ricocheted around the admittedly bad acoustics of the library.

So, the next day, Bill sent JKG a text of his talk, and a week later received a response: "Dear Bill: That was a very pleasant talk you gave about me. If I had known it would be so, I would not have instructed my friend to pretend, in the middle of your speech, to need the attention of a doctor."[50]

Ten years later, Buckley found himself in preparation for Galbraith's 95th birthday party.

James Rosen, a Buckley protégé and editor of *A Torch Kept Lit*, a must-have Buckley publication packed with meticulously selected obituaries of those close to him, tells a story worth remembering, particularly in the context of today's passion-fueled, often ideocratic, political landscape.

Rosen recalls a discussion he had in early 2013 with then-Secretary of State John Kerry asking if the secretary had ever met Buckley. Kerry, a one-time guest on *Firing Line* and—let's not forget—a stout Democrat, said something that would be considered remarkable if it were said in 2025.

"I loved Bill Buckley," he beamed. Upon further inquiry, Kerry cited the ardent Catholic's friendship with the hopelessly liberal J. K. Galbraith as a message and ideal to move toward.

"That's what's missing from politics today,"[50] he wistfully remarked. If only the good secretary knew just how vitriolic it would become thereafter.

Galbraith died April 29, 2006, at the ripe age of ninety-seven. Following his passing, Buckley wrote a love-soaked story of his friendship for *National Review* on May 22 the same year. He wrote, "It pleases me that [Galbraith] knew the value I placed on his friendship, which here impels something of a corruption of my duties." So Buckley recalled the aforementioned metaphor of bailing out sinking ships. In that spirit of barb-edged compliments which gave so much character to their friendship, Buckley continued: "We looked to his writings not for his social indenture to a progressive state, but for the work of a penetrating mind who turned his talent to the service of his ideals."[50]

After a litany of other criticisms of JKG's various political and economic views, Buckley laid out in his own inimitable fashion and in his always-active spirit of Christian love the reminder for readers (and perhaps for himself) that "one needs to brush this aside and dwell on the private life of John Kenneth Galbraith. I know something of that life and of the lengths to which he went in utter privacy to help those in need. He was a truly generous friend. The mighty engine of his intelligence could be marshaled to serve the needs of individual students, students manqué, people who had a problem. Where he would not yield was in intellectual and social perspective."

In the parting passage of the article, Buckley urged the readers of 2006—and perhaps the readers of 2025 onward—to forget "the whole thing, the getting and spending, and the Nobel Prize nominations, and the economists' tributes. What cannot be forgotten by those exposed to them are the amiable, generous, witty interventions of this man, with his singular wife and three remarkable sons, and that is why there are among his friends those who weep that he is now gone."

That's a lesson in civility well worth its weight in gold, and its truth more than lives up to Emerson's dictum to reckon what truly is the "masterpiece of nature."

After Buckley's own shuffle off this mortal coil in 2008 at the similarly ripe age of eight-two, *The New Republic* caught up with JKG's son John, a respected economics professor in his own right, to comment on his late father's relationship with Buckley. "What Bill Buckley once said of my father was equally true of him: He was 'syntactically pure.' Love of language and of the writer's craft bound them together, the left pea to the right. That, and their winter migrations to Switzerland, where the Gstaad Papeterie would signal the arrival of each by placing a book in the window, and where Bill parked his car in our garage. Of my father on skis, he wrote somewhere: 'Like Charles DeGaulle, in an elevator.'"

Because the two had the mutual fondness for exchanging compliments laced with at least one backhand (in the typical way deep friends do), the younger Galbraith noted his father at least once remarking, "Mr. Buckley has a great talent for fiction, as readers of his columns know."

In late June of 1970, at a luncheon address during a conference of New York State Trial Judges, Buckley gave a speech he christened with the curious title "The Republic's Duty to Repress."[90]

It was here Buckley touched on the growing cultural unease about the war in Vietnam with those demanding a withdrawal desiring to engage in "the anarchy passion to smash."

In an anthology of his favorite speeches called *Let Us Talk of Many Things*, Buckley noted these "revolutionists were adamant in their claims. They insisted that the Constitution and its judicial and theoretical evolution guaranteed them absolute rights to proceed with their pursuits, which here and there involved deaths."[90] Here, the good Buckley graced us with a triple tonic of a word against fanaticism, a defense of a friend, and a prescient lesson for the present.

His speech was broken up into several of what he called propositions. Proposition 2 was "The absolutizers, in their struggle against what they call repression, are doing their best to make the Constitution incoherent." After all, one who only thinks in absolutes with no shred of nuance can only be, basically and by definition, a fanatic.

He references the great SCOTUS judge Oliver Wendell Holmes, the same judge who demarcated freedom of speech in terms of whether one may shout fire in a crowded theater in the famous Schenck v. United States case in 1919.

He wrote that Holmes, when asked to define a fanatic, said—and this is of course a paraphrase according to Buckley—"Everyone will agree as a matter of common sense that a house owner owns the space above his roof, so that, for example, he can prevent his neighbor from constructing a perpendicular extension reaching out from his own house to overshadow his neighbors."

According to Buckley, Holmes would say, "The fanatic, however, will reason from his ownership of the space above his roof to ownership of a shaft of air that project[s] straight out into the heavenly spheres, such that no child's kite or supersonic transport can overfly him without written permission." Buckley does go on to recognize the clear irony that it is to Holmes's most famous dissent, that of Schenck v. United States, the fanatics will turn to.

Along with that tonic, Buckley would also serve up a dual helping of a defense of the aforementioned Allard Lowenstein and an admonishment:

"Mr. Lowenstein recently told me that it was not a new experience for him to be silenced, and even threatened and shouted down, by those who disagree with him. But when he was given such treatment by Ku Klux types in the South, the whole of America reacted in horror and registered its solidarity with those who worked for the continuing attrition of the birthmark that the Civil War did not succeed altogether in erasing."[90]

In the same speech, Buckley revealed the staunch antiwar Liberal was "hooted down and literally silenced for defending the right of Professor Herman Kahn to speak unmolested".

Those who incited these furies, according to Buckley, "needless to say went unpunished, even unreprimanded, although they most undisputedly conspired together to abridge the civil liberties of two men, Herman Kahn and Al Lowenstein, who have never by word or deed disparaged the civil liberties of any American citizen."

Can you see, dear reader, the relevance to our current situation in academia and how fanaticism has become so widespread as to become mainstream? I think, perhaps, you can.

The enduring friendship between Buckley and Galbraith, despite the vast delta in their ideals, is a reminder of a now seemingly bygone era of intellectual pluralism. Their barbed but playful exchanges stand in stark contrast to the political landscape of today where any hopes of respectful exchanges are often set aflame by the fires of zealotry.

As we look to the camaraderie they shared, it becomes clear modern society is increasingly lacking an essential element: the ability to engage with opposing ideas without devolving into fanaticism, which could itself be seen as a subspecies of tribalism. If there was a fanatical bone in either of their bodies, their playful disposition while debating would have been all but impossible to assume.

One of the great strengths of the conservative movement of which Buckley was such a notable figure was, it knew how to keep fanatics in check. In particular, Buckley and the whole of *National Review* attacked vociferously the John Birch Society, a supposed exemplar of conservative values. But Buckley saw them as a fringe fanatical group dwelling on the edge (perhaps further) of conspiracy.

For starters, this staunchly anticommunist establishment believed, for instance, Dwight Eisenhower was a communist.

Specifics might best be left for another book, but Buckley once said of its founder, candy tycoon Robert Welch, there doesn't seem to be any level of "lunacy of which [he] isn't capable."

Buckley went on to wonder, in print of course, in August 1965, how anyone in society could take seriously "such paranoid and unpatriotic drivel"[34] as that which emanates from the megaphone of the John Birch Society.

So, one could easily see the salience Buckley put on keeping fanatics in check lest they undermine the broader conservative movement.

They have never quite forgiven him for it. In fact, longtime Bircher John McManus penned his own invective titled "William F. Buckley, Jr.: Pied Piper for the Establishment."

Buckley also valiantly undermined the regrettable Alabama governor George Wallace whom he characterized as effectively a fake conservative who relied on populism. So, it was populism and fanaticism which Buckley proudly waged war against.

Remember, Governor Wallace was the man who infamously said at his January 1963 inaugural address, "Segregation now, segregation tomorrow, segregation forever."

As a historical aside, it could well have been this undermining that prevented Wallace, an unapologetic and avowed segregationist, from securing a place in the White House. After all, far from merely tolerate, he ardently embraced the evils of segregation. We as society are in a clearly unacknowledged debt to Buckley for that act of political chivalry alone.

In an exclusive interview with Rich Lowry, Buckley's friend and the current editor-in-chief of *National Review*, I asked what Buckley might have thought about fanaticism, which is a subspecies of tribalism, and populism today.

Lowry noted, "Buckley had a deep disdain for what he saw as the thoughtlessness of populism."

He elaborated, "He hated Wallace. . . If you look up the *Firing Line* episodes where he discusses Wallace, you'll find his criticism is quite excoriating." Lowry added that

Buckley's aversion was not only to the thoughtlessness of such movements but also to their substance, especially when it conflicted with his market-oriented views.

But in the great spirit of debate of which Buckley is such a notable figure, there was schism and debate within *National Review* over George Wallace.

Lowry explained, "There was a dispute over Wallace within the pages of *National Review*. We had more populist right-wing activists and advocates, like Bill Rusher, who believed we needed a Wallace-type approach—not the racism or anything like that, but a more populist, middle-American approach. They thought we needed those voters to secure a majority."

Lowry contrasted this with Buckley's perspective: "Bill was much more suspicious and reluctant." Lowry also noted Buckley's critique extended beyond populism to include conspiracism, which he saw as deeply poisonous and discrediting to the conservative movement.

"It wasn't that he was against anticommunism," Lowry added. "He just thought anticommunism should be rational. Even though he was a member of it in a way, George Wallace's approach didn't align with Buckley's vision. Buckley had a very dim view of the Eastern elite and was fighting against it, but he wanted to do so in a more credible and intellectual way than Wallace did."

Today, it seems these thoughtless fanatical fringes of both the Left and the Right are, far from being pushed away, being lovingly nestled in the bosom of the moderates to the point where they become indistinguishable.

On the Right, we see those who will proudly and confidently speak of Wayfair conspiracy theories, debunked Pizzagate scandals, adrenochrome, and so on with no authority to install intellectual guardrails off which the sensible moderates can bounce.

On the Left, we see those people who will happily call America a fundamentally and irredeemably white supremacist nation. We perhaps all have seen the spray-painted "AmeriKKKa" adorning many a statue and wall in the wake of the various peaceful protests. Though, I have to comment, none of the purveyors of these vociferous criticisms seem terribly eager to leave this apparently awful country in search of more enlightened and progressive pastures. So, there is perhaps more of that performative, narcissistic element at play here as well.

There is another instance of America's toxic tendency toward fanaticism regarding its odd obsession with race, racism, and responses to it that all seem to emanate from one side of the political aisle, which Douglas Murray cites in his *The War on the West*.

It would be laugh inducing if it weren't, when one gives pause and reflection, so depressing.

Murray makes the correct assessment of Western civilization as one obsessed with the pursuit of knowledge in whatever area knowledge may be attained. Tribalism and the intellectually corrosive effects that come along with it prevent that openness and thirst for knowledge.

Tribalism delivers hammer blows to the very foundations of Western civilization in this way and others.

During the oft-mentioned Summer of Love immediately following the George Floyd scandal in 2020, classical music was—of all things—what wandered into the ever-floating cross-hairs of the scope of tribalism.

Murray makes the aside that this particular pot of water had been on a slow boil since at least 2015 when the *Oxford Handbook* series decided to add a new title to its series. This was, of course, *The Oxford Handbook of Social Justice in Music Education*. If that title was exhausting to read, trust me when I say it was more exhausting to write.

Among the litany of ludicrous prescriptions this handbook presents, it points out that music education in North America was "part of an *obvious* agenda of cultural

Whiteness and that the posture that performers adopt on stage is racist."[13] To whom this would strike as obvious, I am certain I don't know.

Among such predictable cultural prescriptions as reeling back the art of taking musical notation, given (perhaps these are obvious as well) cultural changes, and the obligatory charge to fight existing power structures (which no one can ever really define), is confusing and gorge-rising admonishment to not only teach hip-hop (which is fine) but to "be hip-hop." There is a paradox here Murray calls attention to: given the primacy so many place on the sin of cultural appropriation, how much hip-hop may a white man be before there is blowback?

Pay attention to tribal double-talk of this kind. It is usually revealing.

In any event, the activists of 2020 were working toward equality of both gender and race when it came to increasing their numbers among orchestras and various other classical music groups.

One of the tactics applied for years—which can and in fact is applied to society in general—is the blind audition." The interview panel can only pay special attention to a prospective orchestra member's competency, and there would be no "visual giveaway" as to his or her sex or race.[13]

Correctly, this was touted as a stoutly progressive move, and there was indeed a rise in minority representation in orchestras as a result.

Fast-forward to 2020 and all of a sudden blind auditions have become the problem.

"To Make Orchestras More Diverse, End Blind Auditions," *The New York Times* hollered in print in July of that year.

It was a complete about-face in terms of not only policy but also outlook.

In order for a shot at true diversity—perhaps I can simply say equality?—what simply must be taken into account is "race, gender, and other factors." The same piece rather snidely and in that smug way that seems to occur singularly in the mainstream, journalists wrote that while the policy of blind auditions was "well-intentioned," it now "*impeded* diversity."[35]

Interestingly enough, *The New York Times* rendered a follow-up piece titled "Black Artists on How to Change Classical Music." *The New York Times* couldn't find (and something tells me they were looking quite hard) a single black musician who was in favor of halting these blind auditions.

The National Alliance for Audition Support is, by their own advertisement, an "unprecedented initiative" aimed at increasing the presence and representation by "offering Black and Latinx musicians a customized combination of mentoring, audition preparation, financial support, and audition previews."[36]

This enterprise claims, bizarrely but not surprisingly, that "aspects of our audition/tenure processes continue to contribute to the legacy of systemic racism that has existed in our country since before the very first orchestra was founded."[36]

It goes on to claim, "training in anti-racism, implicit bias and group communication skills are imperative at all levels"[13] in terms of orchestral management and support, Murray goes on to write.

This all speaks to what *The New York Times* has already said: classical music is a "white-dominated field"[35] and thus must be dismantled and transformed like all structures and institutions in American life, up to and including the nuclear family, as organizations like Black Lives Matter proudly proclaimed until they were called out on it. This is where fanaticism lands you in the end. You begin with a tenuous and timid commitment to a broadly appealing and purpose-giving cause, such as the fight against racism, and end at a terminal point of absolute moral and intellectual chaos.

One can see the great onslaught this fanaticism wages on American culture and society. The old liberal trick of labeling something you don't like as racist had, at least at one point, a permanently toxifying effect. It is a sort of moral blackmail that has, in most cases, immunized poisonous ideals such as these against any sort of criticism, as pundits and commentators would have to endlessly—and unfairly—beat back charges of racism.

It isn't helped of course by those chattering ideologies such as Ibram Kendi who once said in a breathtaking example of gaslighting, "I don't think people realize that when they self-identify as 'not racist,' they're essentially identifying in the same way as white supremacists."[37] I don't subscribe to Kendi's "heads I win, tails you lose" approach to race relations, and neither should anyone who happens to flip through these pages.

But this fanatical mode of thought—of simply injecting the accusation of racism, white supremacy, etc.—has infiltrated, as all attacks Western culture invariably will, our literature.

Murray goes on to cite the specific but nonetheless illuminating case of Dr. Vanessa Corredera of Andrew University in Michigan.

It was she who also failed a cultural Rorschach test by claiming, stridently and loudly, all of Shakespeare's plays were, in fact, "race plays" chock-full of what she termed "racialized dynamics."[13] Quite simply, she saw something that wasn't there.

Of Shakespeare's glorious comedy *A Midsummer Night's Dream*, she said, "In context with other plays and even the Sonnets, this language is all over the place, this language of dark and light… these are racializing elements."[13]

But this conclusion can come by way of the anti-intellectual filtration machine on offer by the fanatics of our day.

The New York Post columnist notes, Shakespeare's way with words was generally (dare I say still is by those not given to the bullying of fanatics) admired among scholars. He points out, correctly, what was needed was a dose of "decolonization" and "anti-racism," some of the most worrisome elements borne of that filtration machine. Thus, those who ought to protect the legacy of perhaps the most important writer in the history of the West, certainly the most influential, now had to deal with scholars who are, as Murray beautifully put it, "hostile and inept towards him."[13]

But it was several months earlier when the *School Library Journal* put on a debate discussing the matter of whether the words tumbling out of the Bard of Avon's quill should even be taught or analyzed in American classrooms.

One expert (I wonder what they could possibly be an expert in) said his works were "full of problematic, outdated ideas, with plenty of misogyny, racism, homophobia, classism, anti-Semitism, and misogynoir."[13]

There must surely be a joke lurking somewhere in there about calling works written in the 1500s outdated.

As a relevant thought experiment, if the works are to be "canceled" on the grounds of being racist, does this mean Alex Haley's mainstay *Roots* must be similarly done away with? After all, does *Roots* not dabble in more than its fair share of racism even with the noble goal of making a point of its evil?

Perhaps it's time, for a similar reason, to retire Spielberg's masterpiece *Schindler's List* since, after all, there is plenty of antisemitism to go around in that film. This is a game you could play all day long. But please don't. We all lose.

This black-hole fanaticism will inevitably pull ideals of this kind and is the "anti-thought" that Buckley so heartily raged against.

In a clarion call so typical of these fanatical ideal-ogues, it was concluded the works of *Romeo and Juliet, Taming of the Shrew, MacBeth*, and *Hamlet,* indeed, all of Shakespeare's works—should be "set aside and deemphasized to make room for modern, diverse and inclusive voices."[13]

There may be a slight temptation within you, dear reader, to shrug this off as an isolated incident.

Allow me to give you solace: that is not the case.

It was, Murray goes on to reveal, a former Washington State public school teacher who proudly said she had already extirpated the works of Shakespeare from her classroom.

One can almost feel the virtue through the signal when she revealed her desire to "stray from centering the narrative of white, cisgender, heterosexual men. Eliminating Shakespeare was a step I could easily take to work toward that."[13]

Yet another "educator," this one manning the helm of the English department at a high school in Michigan, proclaimed that teachers have to "challenge the whiteness" of the (one would think harmless and sensible) claim that Shakespeare's works are "universal."[13]

But it isn't just the, so to speak, soft subjects being infected by this cultural virus of tribalism.

It was May 2021 that, of all journals, the scientific magazine *Nature* published a smug editorial on the first anniversary of the death of George Floyd to remind those who must be reminded that "systemic racism in science" is very much with us in the modern world. The same editorial went on to reveal how the staff of *Nature* had to acknowledge their "part in it."[38]

"Racism in science," the editorial went on, "is endemic because the systems that produce and teach scientific knowledge have, for centuries, misrepresented, marginalized and mistreated people of colour and under-represented communities."[38]

"The research system has justified racism—and, too often, scientists in positions of power have benefited from it. That system includes the organization of research: how it is funded, published and evaluated,"[38] the journal whined. The most incurious reader quite quickly notices after even a cursory review of the editorial, the writers rather bravely avoid giving any actual examples of the supposed systemic racism running through the sciences like wildfire. Something to pay attention to always, for what may be argued with no evidence can just as quickly be dismissed without evidence.

It would only amount to a cruel joke if this way of thinking and mode of argument only existed in the fairly useless wilderness of the humanities.

That is, woke or supposedly progressive-minded college students are more than welcome to drive themselves into debt in the pursuit of sharpening their knowledge of lesbian dance theory or turning their gaze to the noble study of Latinx theater at Bucknell University, but that foolishness would surely end once one lands at the doorstep of the hard sciences because quite simply, as Murray notes, "at some point the bridges had to stay up."[13]

But no! The ethic has swarmed through the front door and has taken up residence in the highest reaches of STEM. *That* is the moment it stops being funny and must be dealt with.

While there may have been pockets of subservience to this flavor of dogma, it ran amok, once again, in the immediate aftermath of George Floyd.

You will recall, dear reader, the post-Floyd riots happened in the deepest throws of COVID-induced lockdowns.

These lockdowns were introduced—one may say imposed—largely on the advice of medical "experts."

As an extremely brief refresher, the explanation given to the public for these mandates was to prevent the spread of the coronavirus. So curiously seductive phrases such as *social distancing*, and the practice of keeping a set distance (typically six feet) away from others entered the cultural lexicon.

Well, the ugliest effects of hyper tribalism once again reared their deformed heads when the purveyors of these riots, the now embattled Black Lives Matter organization, began their riots (and, yes, they were riots) across the country. There were over 1000 ideologically captured medical professionals in the most advanced stages of terminal tribalism who put their names—and thus their reputations—on a petition calling people to not only break social distancing but to get out and riot. Why?

The intellectually tepid reason given? Because "'racism and oppression is a public health issue," according to infectious diseases expert Dr. Abby Hussein.

"Staying at home, social distancing, and public masking are effective at minimizing the spread of COVID-19," the letter signers add. "However, as public health advocates, we do not condemn these gatherings as risky for COVID-19 transmission."[39]

Note, first, the language game employed—as it so often is when one examines the magical powers of euphemism—in not calling them riots or even calling them protests, but the rather lame attempt at seeming to be non ideological by using the word *gathering*.

But it gets worse.

The letter expounded, "These protests are 'vital to the national public health and to the threatened health specifically of Black people in the United States.'"[39]

It has to be said, the letter didn't play any further language game of feigned dispassion or indifference. Quite the contrary.

"White supremacy," the letter explained, "is a lethal public health issue that predates and contributes to COVID-19."[39]

Much to delve into there, but I think I'll just let the words stand on their own merit.

The final nail in this intellectual coffin came when these medical professionals wrote, "COVID-19 among Black patients is yet another lethal manifestation of white supremacy."[39]

In a final send-off of both their actual public responsibility of keeping the public safe and, I would argue, their integrity, the signatories to the letter wrote that the "protests against systemic racism, which fosters the disproportionate burden of COVID-19 on Black communities and also perpetuates police violence, must be supported."[39]

But there is an even worse problem on display here. If the medical community is capable of such dramatic, erratic flights from reality, how can they endeavor to be taken seriously as an institution? This is where fanatical devotion to tribalism gets you.

That erosion of integrity has by no means been restored in the aftermath of the lockdown, even assuming we got rid of our post-COVID hangovers. It perhaps has gotten worse.

It was as late as 2023, after all, when Buckley's own *National Review* wrote of how this self-flagellating admission to racism and the perhaps good-hearted but ultimately feckless excursion to course correct (a strategy now know to us as DEI) has infected—pardon the pun—the medical profession.

The article revealed sharp criticism of the American College of Surgeons (ACS) for its adoption of Diversity, Equity, and Inclusion (DEI) principles, claiming these ideologies have no place in medicine. It highlighted the recent launch of a DEI toolkit by the ACS, aimed at promoting antiracism and DEI practices among surgeons but warned such efforts detract from the evidence-based methods traditionally used to improve patient outcomes. Consider, for a moment, selecting a surgeon not on merit but on something as silly as race. Ignoring the obvious racism therein, consider weather this hiring practice is a net positive for public welfare.

The ACS, the article went on to say, is promoting divisive and unproven concepts, such as systemic racism in surgical care; the Implicit Association Test (IAT) to measure racial bias; and the notion that minority patients fare better when treated by doctors of the same race. These claims, it asserted, are based on flawed studies and questionable science. The article expressed concern that by embedding these ideologies into surgical practice, the ACS risks lowering the quality of care and undermining trust in the medical profession.

Furthermore, the article strongly criticized the impact of DEI on surgical education, arguing the introduction of time-consuming ideological training will dilute the rigorous, hands-on experience needed to train competent surgeons. It cited anecdotal evidence from surgical residents who feel they are not receiving sufficient clinical experience while being tasked with learning and adhering to DEI standards.

The article concluded by warning that the ACS's commitment to antiracism and DEI could erode merit-based standards in surgery, jeopardizing patient care and compromising the organization's mission to "Serve All with Skill and Fidelity." The continued promotion of these ideologies, it argued, comes at the peril of the profession and the safety of patients.

A fanatical commitment to toxic ideals was, no doubt, the great fuel powering some of the worst atrocities in human history. Where Buckley saw a person's humanity, ill-fated projects like DEI seek to reduce people simply to their immutable characteristics. A wholly evil endeavor. But it gets worse.

We now live in a society that pathologizes certain races—and one race in particular.

Suspiciously gaslight-infused terms such as *white fragility* and *white rage* have cropped up in both academia and mainstream discourse with frightening frequency, clearing the way for a deep reservoir of fanatical hatred.

One way in which this cancerous mode of thought has metastasized was by way of a course lovingly called "The Problem with Whiteness,"[40] at Arizona State University. This was in 2015, by the way. Long before George Floyd.

Also at ASU, Professor Lee Bebout offers a course titled "U.S. Race Theory & the Problem of Whiteness," which he will teach for the second time in the upcoming semester. The course, which focuses on Critical Whiteness Studies, examines whiteness as a socially constructed concept perpetuating white supremacy. Bebout's syllabus includes works by Toni Morrison, Eduardo Bonilla-Silva (*Racism Without Racists: Color-Blind Racism and the Persistence of Racial Inequality in America*), and Jane H. Hill (*The Everyday Language of White Racism*). Next semester, he will add Ta-Nehisi Coates's *Between the World and Me*.

Bebout, who is white, has faced criticism for the course, with some accusing him of promoting antiwhite sentiments. His work has sparked controversy, particularly after the Campus Reform report. Despite the backlash, Bebout clarifies that the course is not aimed at critiquing white people, but at exploring the systems of racism of privileged whiteness. He stresses that the course is not about vilifying white people but understanding how institutional power works.

This is where that gaslighting comes in. It calls upon students to take a class called "the problem with whiteness,"[40] while saying the class doesn't criticize white people. Another thought experiment: if a person who happened to be white called attention to this glaring issue, would it simply be dismissed as fragility? Or would it perhaps be white rage? You see where this lands you, dear reader. Fanatical commitment, embraced by culture, class, and curriculum, expands into a stifling conformity, quashing legitimate concerns under the guise of moral superiority. This is the very same ideological trap William F. Buckley warned against in his lifelong pursuit of intellectual integrity.

Buckley's commitment to reason and the open exchange of ideas was rooted in the understanding that no idea—no matter how revered—was immune to scrutiny. That is the intellectual and ideological counterpart of OR counterpoint to fanaticism.

He abhorred the sort of ideological orthodoxy that imposed a single narrative, particularly one casting individuals as villains based solely on their background or identity. In Buckley's view, the foundation of a healthy society lies in the ability to engage with differing perspectives, not to cancel or silence them. What we're witnessing today, especially in academic settings, is a distortion of that principle: a culture demands adherence to a single worldview and brands dissent as inherently problematic. In the end, this pursuit of ideological purity leaves us divided, unable to engage in the kind of robust, nuanced conversations essential to a functioning democracy—just as Buckley feared.

This is where we find ourselves today: trapped in a cycle of ideological purity tests demanding conformity, stifling dissent, and ultimately breeding more division. As we witness this cultural shift creeping across various disciplines, from the humanities to the hard sciences, it's clear the battle isn't just about what ideas should be taught. It's about whose voices are allowed to be heard and whose are silenced.

In moments like these, the wisdom of William F. Buckley Jr. becomes all the more crucial. Buckley, a tireless advocate for intellectual diversity and reasoned discourse, rejected the notion that any ideological purity—whether on the Right or the Left—could be allowed to define the parameters of debate. He championed open dialogue not for the sake of appeasing every faction but because he understood genuine progress is achieved through engagement with opposing viewpoints.

Buckley's commitment to the ideals of liberty, to the importance of humility in the face of complexity, and to his refusal to surrender to fanaticism offers a powerful antidote to the ideological purges we see today.

We must resist the temptation to give in to the divisiveness and narrow thinking pervading academia. Instead, we should return to Buckley's example and defend the integrity of institutions by insisting on the free exchange of ideas, a respect for tradition, and a recognition that only through honest, difficult conversation can we hope to overcome the challenges of our time.

CHAPTER 9

George McGovern: Humor

"Say, have I told you about my new best friend? George McGovern! He turns out to be the single nicest human being I've ever met."

This was far from a rebellious or clumsy comment made to Buckley's son Christopher and recounted in his memoir *Losing Mom and Pup*.

It seems so bizarre that not only would Christian love propel Buckley to seek out the friendships he did. But it also seems—particularly when contrasted with the howling wilderness of tribalism pervading society today—he charmed many who were opposed to his ideals yet sought to break bread with him.

The 1972 Democratic presidential hopeful, George McGovern might shine as a particularly bright example of this.

After all, Buckley had at the ready in the pages of *National Review* full columns steadily deployed to their faithful and aimed at the economic and foreign policy views of the South Dakota senator.

The scale of *NR*'s efficacy could well be up for debate, but in the election McGovern was indeed summarily trounced by Richard Nixon in a record landslide.

Despite this, the two would indeed become friends later in their lives. Better than that, they engaged in a debate of ideas as happy warriors multiple times.

It was in 1990, in Lynchburg, Virginia, when the two were to lock horns over the effectiveness of President Bush (the father, of course; not the son) and his administration.

Buckley, who predictably described himself as a radical conservative, addressed the audience of 1,000, explaining why both Bush and his predecessor, Ronald Reagan, were guiding the country in the right direction.

Under their leadership principles, Buckley explained, the Soviet Union began to experience change. He commended Bush for resisting dramatic cuts to the defense budget despite developments in Eastern Europe.

"We don't know what the state of Mr. Gorbachev is, and what we must do is maintain our guard,"[41] said the then-sixty-four-year-old founder and editor of *National Review*.

McGovern, however, criticized Bush for precisely that: "Why is it that we're being offered a military budget the same as last year's as if nothing had happened with the wall coming down in Europe?"[41] According to McGovern, Bush should not be credited for changes in Soviet policy, accusing him of showing "timidity" and "slowness" in responding to the situation.

At sixty-seven, McGovern also took aim at the Bush administration's fiscal policies. He argued that the most urgent issue facing the country was the growing national debt. "It's not a policy simply to say, 'Read my lips,'"[41] McGovern remarked.

In a characteristic exchange between the two, Buckley commented that McGovern's fiscally conservative-sounding advice resembled a "pious disposition" from a Democrat. Despite Reagan's attempts to "squeeze and squeeze" spending, Buckley noted that a Democratic Congress continued to spend.

McGovern turned the tables, labeling Buckley the liberal after Buckley outlined his reasons for advocating drug legalization.

On this topic, the two found themselves closer to agreement than usual. "I'm not 100 percent different,"[41] McGovern admitted, adding that while he had yet to decide on legalization, he currently believed education to be a better solution.

Buckley made light of McGovern's defeat in the 1972 presidential election by Richard Nixon, and McGovern joined in. Despite losing every state except one and the District of Columbia, McGovern humorously pointed out he did, in fact, come in second.

"I'd like to remind my friend, Bill Buckley, he has yet to come in second,"[41] McGovern quipped, referencing Buckley's own failed run for mayor of New York City in 1965, as a candidate for the Conservative Party he helped to establish.

Buckley responded with a jab about McGovern's new career as the owner of a hotel in Stratford, Connecticut. "If 18 years ago he had told me he wanted to be an innkeeper, I could have raised the money overnight,"[41] Buckley retorted.

The whole texture which their debate took seemed symbolic of their friendship. They ardently and unapologetically defended their ideals, but there was always a healthy lacing of humor and good nature—and faith, for that matter—in their words.

McGovern would be one of many who would be in attendance at Buckley's funeral at St. Patrick's Cathedral in New York on April 5, 2008.

It is, in this author's humble estimation, criminally underrated how important a sense of humor is to fostering friendships and serving as an antidote and aid to serious discussion like Buckley and McGovern's debate. There is no better digestive aid to serious points being made than stout helpings of humor.

Humor has been so radically obliterated by tribalism in American society.

The cardinal sin committed today has to be that people of a certain tribal ilk so often equate jokes with values. This is another prime example of a failed cultural Rorschach test. Whereas one person with an overactive imagination could watch Dave Chapelle, for instance, tell a joke involving transgender people and see the seeds of genocidal justification taking root, another will simply see Dave Chapelle tell a joke involving transgender people.

Mainstays on the tube who once fostered a degree of unity—such as *Saturday Night Live* and *The Tonight Show*—now divide with their clear political agenda and obsession to gather "clapter" from the audience rather than having the writing and the humor be at the forefront.

Relative to the sins of tribalism committed by journalism or academia, this may seem a fairly benign transgression, but when we consider the culture and how much our culture does, for better or worse, feed off of television, the implications are far-reaching. When Jimmy Kimmel or Stephen Colbert, for instance, goes after Trump in what's clearly more of an ideological and ill-intended left hook rather than a light-hearted jab, it's a fairly clear indicator who their humor is not for, is it not?

The shift from genuine laughter to clapter-driven responses reflects a broader trend that can't *not* be noticed. Partisanship overshadows the original purpose of entertainment: to bring people together through shared experiences and humor. This shift not only alienates viewers but also creates a fragmented cultural landscape where the lines between entertainment and political messaging blur.

As audiences retreat into echo chambers, the very fabric of community discourse frays. The humor that once served as a bridge between differing perspectives now reinforces divisions, leaving little room for the kind of nuanced dialogue once characterizing late-night television. In this context, the stakes are high. When laughter is weaponized as a political tool, it diminishes our ability to engage with opposing viewpoints and fosters an environment of hostility rather than understanding.

Ultimately, the evolution of shows like *Saturday Night Live* and *The Tonight Show* mirrors a society grappling with polarization: the laughter that once united us now often serves to deepen our divides. Reclaiming the art of comedy as a platform for genuine connection and discourse is essential if we hope to mend the rifts in our cultural conversations.

Contrast this with William F. Buckley and his day when Buckley and Woody Allen could indeed appear on a show together and trade lighthearted jabs at each other with no ill will that all sides enjoyed.

In that 1968 appearance, for instance, an audience member asked Buckley if he liked going to dance clubs, and Allen playfully joked, "Mr. Buckley can't do a dance that was invented after 1860."[42] Buckley's extraordinary response was to simply laugh.

Interestingly enough, another audience member asked Buckley if there were any public figures he would care to name who declined to appear on *Firing Line*.

After a joke about asking Allen several times to appear to no avail, Buckley explained, "Some people don't like to exchange opinions with people who disagree with them sharply because they get used to not being disagreed with. It's sort of an unpleasant sensation to come face-to-face with people who analyze situations differently."[42] The unintended prescience here with regard to modern culture is fairly overwhelming.

As an aside, it has be a sure sign of our intellectual degradation and descent into Mike Judge's aforementioned idiocratical dystopia that intellectuals such as Buckley, Vidal, and Mailer were once mainstays on talk shows, and, as a corollary, the talk shows themselves had the sweet flavor of intellectual seriousness. The heart yearns for a return to Dick Cavett, Mike Douglas, and Johnny Carson.

One can't imagine without at least a chuckle and a head shake, Buckley, for instance, discussing the finer points of Gaza with Jimmy Fallon, can one?

Buckley, Vidal, and Mailer were all on Cavett, sometimes at the same time, and Buckley was on Johnny Carson (where, by the way, he spoke fluent Spanish for the first minute).

This was an era where there were no time-filling games or admittedly charming-in-their-own-way carpool karaokes. There was only serious and enthralling conversation.

Can a culture without humor be a culture worth preserving? Surely not. It seems there is a new depredation every week in this realm calling upon the full force of offense a certain tribe can muster.

Buckley would not have been of the canceling type. He was someone who had the evidently fairly rare ability to see something for what it was. In a 1968 interview, he was asked what he thought of the Warren Beatty mainstay *Bonnie and Clyde*, already infamous at the time of its release for its violence and sex.

Buckley said he thought the movie was "great." He went on to opine there are those, like the interviewer, who had active imaginations and will look at *Bonnie and Clyde* and translate it into, say, American aggressiveness in North Vietnam, whereas other people will simply see a movie where two actors pretend to be gangsters.[10]

A decent prescription here might be to endeavor to live out the latter principle, not the former.

There was a minor controversy back in 2018, when comedian Pete Davidson told a—sorry for the word—offensive joke concerning the Republican congressman from Texas, Dan Crenshaw. The former Navy-Seal-turned-politician lost an eye fighting in Afghanistan, and during the popular "Weekend Update," Davidson said he looked like a "hitman in a porno movie," but he did relent. He knew Crenshaw "lost his eye in war or whatever."

I personally would call the joke in bad taste, which I am perfectly entitled to do within the orbit of my own particular sensibilities without calling for anyone's career to be destroyed. To me, the worst thing about the joke was it was simply bereft of humor, of course, in my opinion.

The salient point here isn't the joke but the response. People seemed desperate to not see the joke as, in fact, a joke, but as a statement and thus worthy of condemnation, showcasing active imaginations once more.

The joke caused the predictable uproar which caused a follow-up appearance from Davidson, this time with a surprise appearance from Crenshaw.

The exchange of jokes and the seemingly heartfelt apology has been immortalized on YouTube, but Crenshaw said something crucial via Twitter (now X) that was available for immediate export and for emulation by all of us.

"Good rule in life: I try hard not to offend; I try harder not to be offended."[43]

So many in our culture these days seem to wake up in the morning anxious to be a victim and anxious to be offended. What a trite and vapid existence it must be.

How much better would our culture become if we as a people agreed to follow Crenshaw's dictum of simply trying to not be offended. 5 percent? 10 percent? More?

I would blush to resort to the actuarial, but let's just say we would see some rather stout and hearty societal returns on that particular investment.

It is also worth pointing out, those who are offended either truly or performatively—and I daresay it is typically performative—are no one's moral superior simply because they're offended.

Comedian Ricky Gervais, well known for his ostensibly offensive humor, put it quite well when he said, "Just because you're offended doesn't mean you're right."

Speaking of comedians, the plight of funnyman Andrew Schultz is also worth diving into. It was he who hosted then-presidential nominee Donald Trump on his *Flagrant* podcast.

He claimed the Brooklyn Academy of Music (BAM) canceled his planned stand-up special just hours after the then-former president's podcast appearance.

The New York comedian explained how he secured shows at BAM over a month in advance but was informed he could no longer perform there just one week before tickets were set to be released.

Here we begin to swim in the always murky waters of a private business or institution's right to run their operation as they see fit. But let's at least acknowledge there was a clear ideological consideration at play that would not have run the other way.

According to Schultz, the cancellation—which he was made aware of via email—came only three hours after the podcast episode aired.

Now, just to do justice to both sides, BAM has denied this. They told the *New York Post*, "It was a prospective rental that was never contracted."[44]

"The decision to pass was made by BAM's senior staff well before the podcast interview with Donald Trump," they added. Perhaps best to leave it to your own judiciousness and judgment, dear reader.

But for true insight on the matter of humor and its degradation in the face of the tribalism in which we find ourselves, I would look to no greater authority than the one and only Jerry Seinfeld.

The comedy icon was interviewed in 2024, while promoting his Netflix movie *Unfrosted* when he railed against the excesses of leftist activists and political correctness, both indicative of a culture overly obsessed with tribalism.

"It used to be you would go home at the end of the day," Seinfield said. "Most people would go, 'Oh, *Cheers* is on, oh, *MASH* is on, *Mary Tyler Moore* is on, *All in the Family* is on.' You just expect that there'll be some funny stuff we can watch on TV tonight," he added. "Guess what?" he asked. "Where is it? Where is it? This is the result of the extreme left and PC crap," he revealed, "and people worrying so much about offending other people."[45]

But he isn't alone. Other famous comedians are with him. Maher and Gervais have come out against this wave of wokeism cascading across our culture.

Maher wrote aptly, "Wokeness started as a great thing, an alert to injustice, and then it morphed into something else. Now it's where common sense goes to die."[46]

Gervais simply bemoaned those who "are fragile and easily offended"[47] by words they disagree with.

The real power of humor, as Buckley would have likely agreed, is that it's funny. No complicated messages required. Humor entertains and, in that laughter, has an unmatched ability to disarm and connect people. It can be an unrivaled weapon in peacekeeping and harmony making.

Lauren Feldman, a professor at Rutgers, echoes this in her recent work, emphasizing comedy's strength is rooted in its ability to bring people together through laughter. Far from a distraction, comedy can be a gateway to deeper thought and perspective precisely because it doesn't demand a serious face to convey ideas.

Feldman's research shows comedy can ease tensions, soften hardened positions, and break down social walls by offering a shared, humorous perspective on issues that might otherwise be too polarizing to discuss. Shows like *Last Week Tonight* and *Black-ish*, for instance, don't browbeat; they entertain and, through that, encourage thought without pushing the audience away. One didn't really need a study to elucidate this point, but scientific backing is never a bad thing.

One example Feldman highlights is how the organization Rise used comedy to push legislative change. When Rise collaborated with *Funny or Die* to make a satirical video, it brought unexpected attention to their cause, helping to pass a significant bill. The success of the video underscores that, when skillfully wielded, humor isn't a cheap distraction but a compelling tool that can draw awareness to issues that might otherwise be ignored. Buckley often used humor as a way to reach audiences across divides, recognizing how wit and irony could convey points with more impact than didactic arguments ever could.

As the pandemic—not so far in our rearview mirror—reminded us, humor also serves as a lifeline, helping people cope with hardship and maintain perspective, such as it was. During the COVID-19 crisis, comedians entertained and offered critique, delivering both relief and insight. Feldman argues, especially in tough times, comedy unites us in shared experience and adds a note of lightness—a principle Buckley might have endorsed as essential to a vibrant culture. He valued humor as a means of finding common ground and connecting with people on human terms.

The Bible, the ceaseless wellspring of wisdom and prescriptions for an ailing culture, echoes the sentiment somewhat in Proverbs 17:22, "A cheerful heart is good medicine, but a crushed spirit dries up the bones." [Bible - 13]

Feldman advises that if advocates and activists want to engage audiences meaningfully, they should respect the craft of comedy and collaborate with professionals who know how to make people laugh, not just relay messages.[48] Genuine humor reaches people precisely because it entertains. As Buckley believed, humor is valuable. At its core, humor is an important thing because it lets us laugh at life and, occasionally, at ourselves. And maybe, just maybe, that laughter is what keeps us sane and civil in the end.

CHAPTER 10

Ira Glasser: Defending Rights and Respect

"Friendship between me and him had seemed out of the question."[49]

Like Ira Glasser, so many of the Left-minded who found themselves in Buckley's orbit seemed to marvel at the fertility of the soil from which a friendship with him would almost invariably take root and blossom.

So, these were words that died on Glasser's lips as it became apparent the head of the then-venerable American Civil Liberties Union (ACLU) indeed found himself in grave danger of becoming friends with Buckley if he wasn't vigilant. He wasn't.

Ira Glasser appeared on *Firing Line* a staggering thirty-four times.

One time—in case anyone was curious what Buckley's thoughts of the ACLU in general were—he and Glasser took part (on opposite sides, of course) in a *Firing Line* episode, recorded on May 4, 1998, titled "Resolved: That the ACLU Is Full of Baloney." There may even be a lesson here for readers: it is OK to crack a joke, and it's also OK for that joke to be at your or my expense.

One story in particular which has lived in written form in many outlets was Glasser's charge that Buckley had no feeling for the experiences of the oft-mentioned but perhaps seldom understood "common man." What followed became a "minor legend within the offices of both the *National Review* and the ACLU." The venture was clear in Glasser's mind as "the beginning of my half-tongue-in-cheek, half-serious effort to acquaint [Buckley] with how ordinary people lived."[49]

It was at the close of one of their debates, appropriately enough, concerning freedom of speech when Glasser, sensing a well-aimed snipe within him, made the charge that Buckley was the "insulated scion of a wealthy family, with no contact with ordinary Americans." Glasser went on to charge—and this was later captured in a piece he wrote for the *Huffington Post*—the *God and Man at Yale* author had no idea what the common people thought or why they thought it, and proposed to take him to lunch one day at Nathan's on Coney Island "instead of the elegant and expensive Manhattan restaurants where he had taken me, if he wanted to get a glimpse of ordinary Americans."

Now, if this conversation were to take place in today's social-media infested hellscape (it is a hellscape for those who seek real discussion), we would see two people trying to performatively grab their X-worthy moment which would likely consist of a flurry of insults and who knows what else.

Buckley not only agreed to the challenge publicly but actually followed through to his great credit (notice there wasn't an iota of performative bravery here), and a few weeks later, they spent a day together. When Buckley was sixty-eight, Glasser took him on his first real subway ride, aside from a ceremonial trip during his 1965 mayoral campaign, to attend his first baseball game: opening day at Shea Stadium between the Mets and the Cubs, 1994.

Jay Nordlinger, longtime *National Review* senior editor and book fellow of the National Review Institute, recalls in his own article in 2017, "Glasser, [the ACLU's] onetime head, was a friend of WFB's. In fact, it was Glasser who took Bill to the only baseball games he ever attended: a Yankees game and a Mets game. (I think Bill was at each game only very briefly.)"[51]

Nordlinger continued: "Glasser made WFB take the subway in order to have a more 'authentic' experience, I suppose. But I'm pretty sure that Bill agreed to take the subway only one way. He went home by his more accustomed means."[51]

"Friendship between me and him had seemed out of the question. We disagreed and fought about everything," Glasser remarked.[49] "More often than not, our debates always became contentious, on virtually every issue: antiterrorism statutes; the death penalty; immigration; school vouchers. Friendship between us seemed a remote fantasy."[49]

But it was, of all issues, drug prohibition that was a bonding agent in their friendship.

Ira Glasser recalled a surprising moment from sometime in the mid- to late-1980s, when he discovered an unexpected ally in William F. Buckley Jr.

"To my surprise, I came across a column in which Buckley had described drug prohibition as a folly and a leading cause of preventable crime," Glasser said. "Relying on his nearly fundamentalist belief in the free market, he argued that given the inevitable and irrepressible demand for drugs and intoxicants, and drawing on the lessons of alcohol prohibition, an unregulated and destructive black market was inevitable, and caused far more harm than it prevented."[49]

Glasser, who had long been a critic of Buckley, was astonished by their newfound common ground.

"Never before having found an issue on which we agreed, I immediately wrote him," Glasser continued. "I told him that he might be equally surprised to know that the ACLU, which he missed no opportunity to denounce and criticize, had taken that very same position for many years."[49]

Glasser proposed they join forces: "I suggested we do something together to advance our common position and that if we did, it might astonish our enemies and amaze our friends."[49]

Following a tour of debates the two did on the topic, Glasser explained how Buckley didn't shy away from opportunities to make clear his alliance with our views. He once publicly characterized *Marijuana Myths, Marijuana Facts: A Review of the Scientific Evidence*, by Glasser's colleagues John Morgan and Lynn Zimmer, as "a miracle of intelligent concision." This made it very difficult for right-wing critics to dismiss the book as liberal propaganda. Probably no one else could have done this as effectively. (And of course a few years ago *National Review* published a terrific article on marijuana prohibition by Ethan Nadelmann as their featured cover story.)[49]

But their collaboration on the subject, Glasser wrote, enriched his life and nurtured their friendship.

Following Buckley's death, Glasser paid him a series of almost lyrical compliments.

Glasser reflected on the ardent Catholic's personal qualities, highlighting what he considered Buckley's most attractive trait.

"One more thing must be said, and it was his most attractive quality," Glasser noted. "He was, on a personal level, an uncommonly kind and gracious man, and a good and loyal friend. I cannot say I was his intimate friend, but in the years I knew him, I saw him on a great many occasions—as a dinner guest, a travel companion, a debating colleague, and an adversary."[49]

Glasser recalled attending numerous social gatherings with Buckley where he observed him enjoying evenings of good food, drink, and spirited discussion. "I saw him with peers, and I saw him with employees. I saw how he behaved with me and how he behaved with my wife. He was, unfailingly, kind, graceful, and attentive."[49]

Glasser contrasted Buckley's rather commanding public persona with his private demeanor. He wrote kindly of Buckley's "unassuming and sensitive nature away from the cameras or the typewriter.

"I have known more than a few people in my decades of public life who took exemplary positions on the abstract questions of human rights, but were terrible people privately. Buckley was the opposite."[49]

Glasser acknowledged his disagreements with many of Buckley's public positions but admired his personal decency. "I deplored many of his public positions and thought their consequences cruel and insensitive, but in private he was wonderful and decent and generous to those around him."[49]

Finally, Glasser reflected on their enduring friendship. "He was, therefore, a good friend in a way I never imagined was possible when we first began our series of public policy debates over 30 years ago. I shall miss him."[49]

Bravo, Buckley and Glasser! That is friendship amid disagreement which we should all aspire to.

To linger just for a little bit on whether the ACLU is indeed full of baloney, it has at this point been made rotten by the poisons of identity politics and ideological capture.

The ACLU was an organization that fully merited bipartisan attention and due seriousness. Their absolute commitment to freedom of speech and the necessity to defend even odious opinions should be the common cause of all Americans.

In fact, the curious observer here might do well to look up the infamous example of Skokie, Illinois, where in 1977, the ACLU of Illinois was contacted by a Nazi leader (you read that correctly: the Nazis called upon the ACLU for redress) who complained their proposed demonstration in the heavily Jewish city of Skokie was obstructed.

The following legal battle, along with the controversy it sparked, challenged the organization's dedication to upholding the First Amendment.

The ACLU does not have to, nor should anyone, defend the Nazis' opinions or actions here. They did well in understanding their obligation to defend the Nazis' right to hold them. Here, we must cloak ourselves in Voltairian cloth by simply understanding that while we may not agree with what someone says, we ought to defend to the death one's right to say it. It must include the right (and ideally gumption) to defend the opinions of those whom we might find utterly repugnant.

It was all sublimely captured by then-National Executive Director Aryeh Neier in his book *Defending My Enemy: Skokie and the Legacy of Free Speech in America*. The ACLU, at least at that moment in history, stood for freedom of speech to the point they would defend the Nazis' right to be heard.

Fast-forward to modern times, and we will simply have to admit with scorn that the ACLU has become ideologically captured.

Such is the pain and penalty of living in the polarized time of our day when all must find their tribe, people, and institutions alike, like iron filings mindlessly obeying the magnet.

The ACLU now attempt a rather obvious sleight of hand where they will advise, quite boldly, they don't "endorse or oppose candidates for elected office." To advertise that sort of supposed dispassion and non-bias while also demanding Project 2025 be stopped, that the extirpation of unborn children is a right and one that demands full attention and support, as well as that "America was founded on White supremacy" is having it both ways in the most promiscuous and exorbitant manner.[52]

Their clear bias falls distinctly Left, which might be fine, but that is not the banner under which the ACLU advertises

Far be it from me to shove words into the mouth of Mr. Glasser, but I strongly suspect he wouldn't exactly disagree with me. In fact, I don't even have to speculate on this point. After all, when asked by host Bill Maher in 2022, if the ACLU is still the stalwart defender of free speech, Glasser—who was at the helm—simply grimaced: "Not as much."[53]

Worse than that, Glasser revealed the institution had, a few years earlier, produced new requirements for its legal team to reference when determining which cases to take up arms for or against.

Fair enough. Only so many hours in the day and only so many causes one can battle at a given time.

But Glasser further revealed, shockingly, that the guidelines in effect are meant to help the attorneys discern which of those free speech cases may not be offensive or threatening to "other civil liberties values."

"In other words, before they're gonna defend your free speech, they want to see what you say," he remarked.[53]

Who could have summoned in their mind a more horrifying picture of an ideologically captured institution.

It must not be forgotten, America is not a democracy. Democracy is simply the tyranny of the majority. America is a constitutional republic. In fact, the embryonic form the word *democrat* took simply meant "someone who was in favor of mob rule."

The ACLU has—in my and apparently in Mr. Glasser's judgment—become a benighted institution. Darkness, the kind that tends to crop up when the light of the Christian ethic has been blown out like a candle on a windy night, has simply descended.

Evil is very much like cold in that way. Cold isn't something that radiates. Cold is the absence of heat. Thus, the darkness of evil proliferates, as Buckley would opine, when the radiating glow of Christian love and warmth has been bled out of the culture.

I mentioned this captured institution asserts abortions are a human right, fully worthy of moral and legal protection—and this in the vast wilderness of social and civil causes the ACLU could commit their time and energy to. And recall, the ACLU now apparently thumbs their noses at free speech cases with which they happen to ideologically part company. They've instead chosen to prioritize defending abortion under the guise of "pregnancy-related care." Rather than focus on true worker protections, the ACLU—as of this writing—has been pushing for the Pregnant Workers Fairness Act to include abortion accommodations, framing it as essential care.

This is the minefield of euphemism and double-talk often awaiting those who venture into this type of territory.

But this so-called "care" strips unborn children of their lives and forces employers to comply with policies that undermine the sanctity of life. By standing with the

Equal Employment Opportunity Commission's (EEOC) regulations, the ACLU is advocating for a society where abortion is treated as an unavoidable right at the expense of moral values and the protection of the unborn. This isn't about fairness; it's about pushing an extreme agenda that values political ideology over life itself.

John Williams, legal director of the ACLU of Arkansas, doesn't seem to disagree with me: "The Pregnant Workers Fairness Act and its regulations provide a lifeline for workers who need accommodations during the most critical periods of their lives. Attempting to strip away these protections, particularly for abortion-related needs, is an affront to the rights and well-being of pregnant workers. . . . All people in all aspects of pregnancy, including abortion, should be treated with the care and consideration they deserve. We stand firmly with the EEOC in defending these essential protections."[54]

Now I won't resort to cliché here by sanctimoniously asking why those protections don't extend to the unborn child, but if we live in a culture filled with morally devolving institutions like the ACLU that, in its present form, will happily work toward the massacre of children, what sort of future are we working toward?

Now let's suppose it is a pro-choice person who is thumbing through these pages.

Assuming you haven't already chucked this book in the trash in anger, I would urge you to please don't get caught in the semantic quicksand that can so often emerge where the forest gets missed for the trees.

The point here is, there is an organization that isn't what it says it is when it holds itself out as a cold, dispassionate warrior against the abuses of civil liberties, wherever those abuses may be.

The ACLU extols its purpose as to realize the "promise of the United States Constitution for all and expand the reach of its guarantees."[52] The fact is, it has become so ideologically captured and beholden to the tyranny of perhaps not even the majority (though that would be anyone's debate) but to the tyranny of a distinctly raucous and loud minority no doubt amplified by the idiocratic-producing hysteria of social media.

We bemoan benighted and ideologically imprisoned institutions that have stepped away from the basking glow of the Holy Light, and another civil rights powerhouse—the Southern Poverty Law Center (SPLC)—has fallen into the same ideological trap.

The SPLC describes themselves as fully committed to "eradicating . . . inequality."[56] Sounds noble enough on its face, but they make the same category error the ACLU does: in as they endeavor to supposedly bridge divides, all they do is pour large canisters of gasoline on an already uncontrollable social wildfire.

The SPLC makes the rather nebulous idea of combating inequality central to its ethic and maintains a movement toward universal equality is the antidote to evil in the world.

The Marxist ideal of utopias is a strange concept indeed. They are often incorrectly perceived as a romantic illusion. They're North Stars we should endeavor to always sail toward but never fully dock. In other words, the ideal might not intersect (pardon the fashionable term) with reality in the most necessary way, but in striving toward it, we are farther ahead in our position than if we hadn't. This is piffle. Sinister piffle.

Utopias are poisonous delusions. When they are taken in combination with the natural tendencies of mankind—those of innovation and enterprise which will by their nature create inequality in society—the distance between the delusion and the reality will often lead to the sanguinary conflicts so well known in history.

The poisonous delusions must be recognized as such.

Thus, to advertise one's voluntary conscription into battle for lofty and nebulous equality, one shows their cards and indeed perhaps their ideals.

Buckley said in one of those infamous debates with Gore Vidal back in 1968, "Freedom breeds inequality."

Vidal, sensing an impending rhetorical knockout, demanded Buckley repeat it a second time.

"Freedom breeds inequality! I'll say it a third time," Buckley shot back.

From beyond the grave, Buckley calls to my mind that paradoxical line from Orwell's *Animal Farm*: "All animals are equal. But some animals are more equal than others."[57]

To put a razor-sharp point on it, the 1662 Book of Common Prayer (oddly enough, Christopher Hitchens's fervently Christian brother Peter quoted to me some years back) reminds us, "God, the author of peace and lover of concord, to know [Him] is eternal life and to serve [Him] is perfect freedom."[58]

If people are left to their own authority, their own ideals, and their own adventures, doesn't that immediately cement in the reasonable thinker's mind that inequality is inevitable by dint of action and outcome if we live by the light of the Lord and strive toward perfect freedom?

This moral and intellectual confusion is among the charges I wish to levy against the SPLC.

Additionally, there is the rather nasty tendency too often observed in our culture where now-common name calling—"Nazi," "white supremacist," "racist," you can add to this for yourself—far too often characterizes the utterances of anyone on the receiving end of an unhappy disagreement.

My charge is, the SPLC has contributed to intellectual stagnation in discourse by simply characterizing those who disagree with certain presuppositions as racists and white supremacists.

Recall to your mind, dear reader, the curious case of Maajid Nawaz.

He is a former radical Muslim who has since apostatized from the so-called Religion of Peace and now speaks as a staunch critic against extremism and fundamentalism, calling for an inoculation of secularism among those touched by Allah with Muhammad as his messenger.

Irony abounds in what would seem to fit the mold of a role model for an SPLC-adjacent ideological figure. That is, one who doesn't live by the lights of fanaticism and extremism but calls attention to it as an unkind observer. The problem, it turned out, was the particular ideology Maajid Nawaz sought to criticize.

Thus, one could imagine the good activist's shock when he found himself on a certain list put out by the SPLC in 2016, marking him as one in a cadre of supposed "anti-Muslim extremists."[59]

There was simply no undertaking to understand what he actually thought. The SPLC heartily rushed to judgment, and of course that judgment was to the benefit of their various ideological echo chambers.

There is so much to aim at here. Even the most well-intentioned snipers know not quite where to begin. Perhaps it fits right into the larger cultural narrative that any criticism whatsoever of the Religion of Peace may be conflated to bigotry against practicing Muslims.

That moral confusion does not take place in any other domain of theological or ideological criticism.

If one were to criticize perhaps St. Augustine of Hippo's declaration that unbaptized babies were doomed to a sort of celestial waiting room known to the Holy See as Purgatory, would it not be crystal clear it is an ideal and not a person being criticized? One would rather clearly be criticizing Catholicism, not a Catholic.

But, alas, Nawaz found himself suddenly in league—by means of his entrance into the list—with the Ku Klux Klan, neo-Nazi groups, and a wide range of radioactive company. Now, I must inject the caveat, after a lawsuit, the SPLC did remove him and had to shell out almost $3.5 million as a result.

But it isn't just Islam. Readers can, I suspect, quickly call to the front of their mind their own favorite example of an ideological clique that should be, needs to be, in fact must be criticized, but they don't dare do so for fear of social ostracization.

These cliques undoubtedly dominated the Left side of the political discussion if only by virtue of the fact it has been primarily they who have infiltrated and dominated academia and journalism, just for a start.

Additionally, of course, the expulsion of God from these institutions and society in general has created a moral void, one filled not with reason or debate but too often dominated by the dogma of identity politics and a rigid secular orthodoxy. This was exactly the kind of stuff Buckley aimed his own sniper rifle at over seventy years ago with *God and Man at Yale*.

But how did we get these toxifying effects on such a grand scale?

How did we get to a place in time and culture where simply criticizing an ideal is an intolerable revolutionary act and one that comes with consequences?

That is the delta that can be redressed with a return to marching stridently toward a culture's perfect freedom. That is the software program I would encourage the SPLC and many other such institutions to download onto their moral hard drive.

We have to hold to, as a society, the firm and unyielding belief that not only is no institution above criticism (including especially barbed criticism), but any organization or institute that holds itself as above and immune to criticism almost by definition demands unkind scrutiny from a less-than-timid, less-than-polite observer.

Be it Islam or whatever taboo institution you'd like to fill your mind with, have these institutions and the poisoned ideological presuppositions guiding them contributed to the heightened tribalism so preoccupying our society? I daresay they have.

Perhaps the moral and intellectual admonishment here is for a true understanding of ideals and each other without the beer goggles of ideological fanaticism. That understanding comes to an open heart, an open mind, and an orientation toward understanding.

Were Buckley here to offer his sage Catholic counsel, he might encourage us to heartily whistle past the ideological graveyard of poisonous delusions of equality and might well invoke the lesson of Proverbs 18:12—"Fools find no pleasure in understanding but delight in airing their own opinions."

CHAPTER 11

Whittaker Chambers: A Conservative's Reconciliation

Rich Lowry, in my interview with him, remarked on the "idiosyncratic" nature of Buckley. The curious case of Al Lowenstein was at the center of our discussion, but there are a few bricks of idiosyncrasy built into the very foundation of *National Review*.

It also speaks to Buckley's capacity for the most noble form of forgiveness, that of the heart. He could recognize when someone underwent a genuine transformation. Buckley saw a changed soul and, crucially, could proceed without holding a person's past against them.

It may seem cliché and pedantic to call upon the Bible to elucidate the point of forgiveness, but Luke 6:37 speaks to the point perfectly: "Do not judge, and you will not be judged. Do not condemn, and you will not be condemned. Forgive, and you will be forgiven." [Bible - 14] Permit me then, dear reader, to christen this sentiment, simply, forgiveness from the heart.

That two ardent communists, albeit reformed, served as founding members of *National Review*, despite Buckley's hatred of the blood-stained ideology, seemed perfectly Buckleyesque.

One saw in *NR*'s founding the one time Trotskyist James Burnham as well as Frank S. Meyer, the man who would develop the political theory of "fusionism" and former a Communist Party USA apparatchik (full-time communist functionary) who would go on to serve as the magazine's book and cultural editor.

Though he wasn't a founding member, none would do more to bolster Buckley's reputation for this particular flavor of forgiveness on the matter of reformation as much as the mysterious and rather mob like visage of communist-spy-turned-editor Whittaker Chambers.

It was nearly eighty years ago, on August 3, 1948, when Chambers, then a forty-seven-year-old senior editor at *Time Magazine* gave an earth-shattering testimony before the infamous and much-maligned House Committee on Un-American Activities or HUAC. A move which prompted Buckley to label Chambers as "the most important American defector from Communism."

It was here Chambers revealed that in the 1930s, he helped organize what Carl Bogus calls in his book, *Buckley: William F. Buckley Jr and the Rise of American Conservatism*, "an underground communist apparatus" and assisted in operating "a secret cell that had infiltrated the American Government."

During the 1930s, Chambers worked as a spy for Soviet military intelligence, establishing a communist espionage network in Washington, DC, which included several journalists and federal officials during the New Deal era.

This network supplied Chambers with copies of government documents, reports, and plans, which he then passed on to Soviet intelligence operatives.

In 1938, Chambers left the blood-stained ideology of communism behind following a significant Christian conversion, which deepened his understanding of how communist ideology persecuted and undermined the human spirit.

One would think his former love of communism alone would soak Chambers in irredeemable anathema where Buckley was concerned. It mustn't be forgotten, Buckley was a virulent and—one might be able to keep their dignity while uttering the word— fanatical supporter of anti-communism and the smorgasbord of fear and paranoia from which his friend, Senator Joseph McCarthy and his ilk so richly dined. The hatred Buckley felt for communism couldn't really be overstated, in this author's humble judgment.

But, having named and implicated himself publicly in this plot, he read the names of seven other members of the cell, one of whom was the now-infamous Alger Hiss. The subsequent skirmishes at the HUAC might well comprise—indeed, have comprised—their own books.

Chambers would go on to pen his memoir, *Witness*, in 1952, where he wrote "The simple fact is that when I took up my little sling and aimed at Communism, I also hit something else. What I hit was the forces of that great socialist revolution, which, in the name of liberalism, spasmodically, incompletely, somewhat formlessly, but always in the same direction, has been inching its ice cap over the nation for two decades."[60]

Witness was a massive bestseller and is considered by many essential reading in the world of conservatism along with Russell Kirk's *The Conservative Mind: From Burke to Eliot* and (nominally) Barry Goldwater's *The Conscience of a Conservative,* seminal pieces of the movement.

"I was shaken by that book [*Witness*]," Buckley exclaimed. "I wasn't shaken into a position I hadn't already occupied, but if possible I felt more passionate about the responsibilities of people who dissented against a particular trend in Western history."[61] That seems to be the height of praise from someone who would, in the course of his lifetime, pen fifty-six books ranging from his sailing books and best-selling spy novels to, of course his political tomes.

The topic of communism or perhaps anticommunism is the perfect topic for Buckley and Chambers to circle around. In December of 1953, rightly vilified Senator McCarthy was given a what-you-might-call pre-release of Buckley's book (penned in cooperation with L. Brent Bozell) *McCarthy and His Enemies: The Record and Its Meaning*, which would be published the following March. Senator McCarthy, to keep a long story short, was concerned the book—a supposed defense of McCarthyism—would do net damage. Chambers couldn't help himself.

"Dear Henry," Chambers wrote in a letter in January 1951, to publisher Henry Regnery, "please take my order for the co-author's book right away. In my opinion," he went on, "the Senator hasn't got a leg to stand on. I don't see how, in the end, he can fail to realize that the book does him the great service of stating his case with understanding, clarity, cogency, good humor, knowingness and more generosity than any would be inclined to indulge simply on the face of some of the cited facts.

"Besides, the authors managed to make it readable from start to end. This is a feat."

So, by their mutual admissions or perhaps assertions, they both had a fondness for the other's books. However, Buckley upon learning of Chambers's letter, wired him to ask of his willingness to produce a blurb on the book for promotional use. In summary, Chambers declined but wrote Buckley in early February 1954, that he was "deeply concerned" about offending or wounding the former Army captain by way of his refusal. Chambers went on a rampage in the letter setting about why he "cannot move in the McCarthy controversy even by endorsing publicly a book which is of necessity a function of that controversy."[62]

So, that was how Buckley found Chambers. He stood in the admittedly vague but nonetheless vaunted role of rebellious dissenter.

In a 1993 interview with Brian Lamb on Buckley's somewhat confusingly titled thirty-fifth book *Happy Days Were Here Again: Reflections of a Libertarian Journalist*, Lamb asked Buckley if he knew which among his cadre of friends and acquaintances he quoted and talked about the most in the book.

"No, I don't," Buckley answered. Indeed, it was Whittaker Chambers, Lamb explained.

The conservative (or is it libertarian now?) Buckley said he and Chambers were great friends for a shade under a decade. He also noted a great love for the kind letters exchanged between him and Chambers, calling out what was written and the way they were written.

Buckley wrote in his autobiography *Miles Gone By* that after meeting Chambers at his farm in 1954, they became friends. He wrote of Chambers's "mysterious humor" and "instant communicability of his overwhelming personal tenderness."[24]

No doubt the Catholic ambition to appreciate penitence combined with the equally Christian virtue of forgiveness fed into Buckley's decision to ultimately hire, in early 1957, and six months after Eisenhower won his reelection, Chambers as a senior editor for a new conservative magazine he was starting, first called *Weekly Review*, then finally *National Review*.

When the ex-spy did finally join after some legendary cajoling by Buckley, he was situated on the third floor of the New York office overlooking a debris-ridden courtyard. Imagine Chambers's surprise when another tenant, who was soon to be vacating the eighth floor of the same building, heartily chucked his old bedsprings out the window, sending them sailing past his.

If there was one bonding agent between Buckley and Chambers, it would have to be their shared understanding of the evils of Marxism and of the full realization of Marxism: communism.

Indeed, Chambers, in an article for *NR* published in 1957, wrote that the great theoretical developments in the world are "argued, heatedly within Western socialism, violently within Communism."[63]

It was March 16, 1960, a little over a year before Chambers's death, when he wrote to Buckley: "You have just done something kind for me. Something that was so timely and word of which reached me in so odd a way, that I want to ramble back and tell you how it used to be."[62]

Chambers relayed how on the street where he grew up, there was forever a Methodist Episcopal minister who lived around him. As he put it, the minister "lived on our street, a block above, or, later, next door, though across a wide lot, now a boulevard."

In the letter, Chambers cites first a Reverend Mr. Glover, whom he admitted to not remembering at all, though he did strike up a friendship with the good reverend's son, who once accompanied him to a downed oil freighter at Long Beach where the two collected "washed up 10 gallon cans" and, as Chambers put it, "upped the Methodist Episcopal income."

He also expressed fondness for Mrs. Glover and their daughter as it was at the little girl's birthday party he "became sicker than [he] had ever been" and would next be struck down by scarlet fever.

But there was another "ME divine" whom Chambers opts to "leave unsung" in the letter.

Reverend Grover and his life seemed quite the opposite, according to Chambers's letter.

He was, as Chambers so wistfully put it, "a big loud-mouthed, assertive, fungoid man, whose unhappy wife regularly presented him with a baby as soon as she was able to totter about after the one just before."

Finally, Chambers brought to light a third man of the cloth from his childhood.

"He was the Rev. Mr. Adams."

"He was," Chambers wrote, "a quiet, thin, slightly stooped, white-haired man, of a mild but most dignified face; dressed in a dark suit, which I recollect as being longer in the jacket than the style was."

"He made a great impression on me," Chambers revealed.

"I thought: this is what a minister should be," the former spy went on.

The *Witness* author wrote, the preacher's wife was "also quiet and dignified," though at this point she was simply a faded fragment of a memory.

But the two had a daughter, Josephine Adams, whom he thought of as a grown-up when he was only twelve. He wrote in the letter to Buckley how he couldn't quite place why he remembered her so well. She has some "intangible quality" cementing her in his mind.

It was after Chambers's book *Witness* appeared, he revealed in the letter, he received a "generous and moving letter" from young Adams. She was, according to Chambers, "caught by [his] evocation of Long Island in those days before the War."

But Chambers relayed that the day before he sent this letter to Buckley, he was once again written to by Josephine Adams.

Addressing Buckley (of course) in the letter, he wrote, "She had heard you on Mike Wallace's show. Wallace had asked you a question and you had answered with my name.

"She then went on to express her pleasure at what you said. She went on to ask if you might send me *Up from Liberalism*, which she meant to ask you to autograph.

"Here I want only to touch on what you did and said.

"In the past," Chambers wrote appreciatively, "you have done and said much, a great deal, for which I have been grateful, and not good at saying how much.

"But there are moments when what is said and done is given an exceptional force by the moment's context, even if sayer or doer does not know it, does not know what moment it is he has brushed.

"I had reached one of those moments," Chambers remarked.

"I don't want to get too much into it," Chambers explained, somewhat paradoxically.

"It was such a moment as one says in: 'I am absolutely alone; I have given everything I had to give, and there is nothing.'

"I do not wish to justify this moment or this feeling; only to note that it existed. You swept me out of this moment. I am grateful. I'm going to leave it there."

He transitioned in the letter to a recent lunch he had with Richard Nixon where he came away "most unhappy" with feelings of "dismay and gnawing pity" washing over him in a tidal wave. He felt Nixon was "asking to assume the first post of danger at the moment of the most fearful and (at least) semi-final stages of the transitions from the older age to the new."

"I believe he is the best there is," Chambers revealed. "I am not sure that is enough, the odds being so great."[62]

Context is always helpful, and here it is well worth pointing out that in March 1960, (when the letter was penned) Nixon was the sitting vice president of the United States under President Dwight D. Eisenhower. At that time, he was also the presumptive Republican nominee for the 1960 presidential election. Nixon announced his candidacy for president in January of that year and was preparing for what would become a highly competitive race against Democratic Senator John F. Kennedy. Nixon was seen as the natural successor to Eisenhower, enjoying broad support within the Republican Party.

He of course—perhaps because of one infamously sweaty debate performance against Kennedy—did not reach the highest office in 1960, and wouldn't ascend to it until January 20, 1969.

Buckley and Chambers planned to spend Easter together in Camden, South Carolina, at Buckley's mother's house. Buckley expressed Chambers's excitement at the prospects of the trip but, alas, a week before they were meant to leave, Chambers sent him a telegram "canceling everything."

It was April 9, 1961, three months to the day before Chambers's death that he sent one last letter to Buckley.

"You meant to do something generous and beautiful, and we seemed to dash it back in your face," Chambers lamented.

"Weariness, Bill—you cannot yet know literally what it means. I wish no time would come when you do know, but the balance of experience is against it. One day, long hence, you will know true weariness and will say: 'That was it.'

"My own life of late has been full of such realizations: 'So *that* was why he did that'; 'So *that* was why she didn't do that'; about the past acts of people whom my own age (and hence understanding) has only just caught up with."

Chambers wrote, "There's a kind of pathos about it—a rather empty kind, I'm afraid; the understanding comes too late to do even the tardy understanding much good."[62]

The old spy went on to say their trip struck him as "completely impromptu," but he "hadn't understood."

While Chambers offered a firm purpose of amendment and apology, he did concede, "I think we spared you a lot of nuisance."

With a note about stoicism, he lamented they never complained of the weariness but that one "should take good care not to inflict [the weariness] on other people's lives," saying that was, in fact, what he did for Buckley. "I'm sorry about that."

It was on July 9, 1961, when fate ordained the man who once fought so fiercely in the battle of ideals would now rest in peace, his journey complete. He was, after all, in 1984, posthumously awarded the Presidential Medal of Freedom by Ronald Reagan for his contribution to "the century's epic struggle between freedom and totalitarianism." The words of the great Arthur Koestler comprised his epitaph: "The witness is gone. The testimony will stand."

Buckley had just finished his weekly editorial lunch at *National Review* and made his way to his office where a phone call was waiting for him.

It was Whittaker's son, John.

"A heart attack. The final heart attack," Buckley wrote of the interchange.

The press was alerted later that afternoon.

"I mumbled the usual inappropriate things, hung up the telephone, sat down, and wept," Buckley admitted.[24]

Buckley's ability to overlook the past and perhaps toxic affiliations people he knew had was and still is a rather undervalued character asset.

It is crucially important to remember certainly in today's society that while to err is human, forgiveness is indeed divine.

Buckley held steadfast to the lesson of Ephesians 4:32: "Be kind and compassionate to one another, forgiving each other, just as in Christ God forgave you." [Bible - 15]

Forgiveness does seem to be a Christian ethic largely bled out of our culture. There seems to be a societal illness that has emerged: celebrating the act of canceling and, more disturbingly, canceling forever.

Buckley's capacity for forgiveness of the heart stands in stark contrast to this trend. While modern culture often seeks permanent condemnation for past sins, Buckley believed in redemption. He knew transformation and the willingness to turn away from past mistakes deserved recognition, not perpetual punishment.

In a society increasingly divided, the act of forgiveness has never been more crucial. It is a value often overlooked today, but it holds the power to heal not just individuals but entire communities. Forgiveness is not a mere relinquishing of grievances but a deeper choice to extend grace, rooted in understanding and compassion. It's about recognizing we all fall short and redemption, through mercy, is a possibility for everyone.

At a time when so much of our public discourse is shaped by anger and division, forgiveness offers a transformative path forward. It enables us to look beyond offenses and see the humanity of one another. It's a refusal to be imprisoned by bitterness and a willingness to see others not for their mistakes but for their potential to change.

In this regard, Buckley's life and work stand as a powerful example. Known for his sharp intellect and forthright opinions, Buckley was not easily swayed. Yet even in his most contentious debates, he practiced forgiveness as a reflection of his Christian faith. His deep commitment to Christianity was the wellspring of his ability to forgive those with whom he disagreed even when their differences were profound. It was not weakness but strength that allowed Buckley to forgive, for he understood true strength is rooted in grace.

Today, we are witnessing a culture often choosing the path of canceling, shaming, and severing ties. The impulse to hold onto offenses, to demand retribution, leaves no room for growth, for transformation. But what if, instead, we extended the kind of forgiveness Buckley modeled?

What if we as a society ran the Buckley program—as someone who understood forgiveness is a reflection of Christ's love and a necessary step toward healing? Buckley's own faith underpinned his willingness to forgive, and through this lens of Christian charity, he was able to reconcile even with those who had once opposed him.

Forgiveness is not about excusing wrongdoing or pretending harm didn't happen. It is about choosing to move forward—both for our own peace and for the restoration of the community. It's about building bridges instead of walls and offering a second chance when it is needed most. In a world filled with divisions, the Christian practice of forgiveness could be the unifying force we so desperately need. Buckley's life demonstrates forgiveness is not a mere ideal, but a powerful tool to create a more just, merciful, and reconciled society. If we could all adopt this way of living, perhaps we could begin to heal the rifts separating us and create a world that reflects the compassion Christ calls us to show one another.

We all want to live in a society that encourages forgiveness. That we currently don't is a blight working against all of us. I want to be able to honestly and quickly forgive someone who needs it. But also, perhaps selfishly, I want to live in a society where my own apology for some depredation that will no doubt be committed in the future is heeded and granted. Thus, a society that does not encourage forgiveness—as well as insisting on its corollary, the apology—is a sure sign of diminished intellectual and moral vitality.

"Forgiveness," Mark Twain famously wrote, "is the fragrance that the violet sheds on the heel that has crushed it."

I say, let that sweet fragrance waft in the air like the finest Parisian perfume.

Speaking of asking for forgiveness…

CHAPTER 12

Including Me

Mea maxima culpa.

This is an old Latin phrase which translates roughly to "through my most grievous fault."

It is part of the Roman Catholic prayer of confession, and the phrase doubtlessly passed through Buckley's lips innumerable times throughout his life.

Out of that grand Christian tradition of confession, coupled with the equally solemn Christian virtue of penitence, I want to address my *mea maxima culpa* directly to you, dear reader.

I'll get on with it shortly, but only briefly want to share my reason for insisting on this chapter of my humble Buckley tome.

It is pathetically easy to call for healing, dialing down the temperature, bringing down the rhetoric—pick your own tired and pointless clichéd call to unity. I say it's pointless because no one—least of all those enjoying the spoils of political office who most need to—says the point-activating line which should follow axiomatically: ". . . including me."

Many people across the political spectrum seem to view calls to be forgiven like they do prisons or hell, in that they're meant for other people.

We all—*including me*—need to work stridently to return to civility in our day.

So, my penitent offering for your consideration is to run through specifically how I have contributed, in print, to the fragmentation pervading society today and where my own vocal setting was dialed far past eleven and certainly far past what would be appropriate.

Deep breath, Cohen.

Off I go . . .

My writing career took off when I was noticed by a controversial journalist and commentator named Laura Loomer. Her name will likely be known to at least some of you. She read some articles I penned on my blog—ranging from imprisoned Czechoslovakian playwright Vaclav Havel (no clue why that article never caught on) and my experiences interviewing alleged Clinton victim Juanita Broaddrick—and thought enough of them to offer me a job writing for her news website.

I was ecstatic!

The chance to actually be a staff writer (though it was freelance) and to contribute articles like those I have admired so passionately—vis-à-vis Buckley and Hitchens—felt like a dream come true. As an aside, I will forever be grateful to you for that opportunity, Laura.

She praised my work often which was a similar tonic for my ego. To receive approbation from a public figure, even one as—pardon the never-ending echo of the word—polarizing as Loomer, meant the world and perhaps the galaxy to a nervous young writer trying to scribble his way to the top.

The first article I wrote, published *way* back in 2019, (note my quite deliberate attempt to distance myself from the piece), focused on the proliferation of Islam in America, specifically the Muslim-majority Michigan cities of Dearborn and Hamtramck. There is, no doubt, a good-faith discussion to have on the point of cultural clashes or what is perceived as such, but I won't be venturing into that domain of debate. At least not in this book.

I also exhibited a weakness in my still-developing journalistic ethic for confirmation bias as well as a regrettable tendency to lean right (pun definitely intended) into fringe domains of conspiratorial thinking. In the same piece, I referenced a document known as the "Explanatory Memorandum." I'll let you research and decide how fringe it is—or even if it is at all —but if I had it to do over again, I would insist on a second source and a vocal setting of perhaps a five. *Mea culpa*.

Because comedy comes in threes, my biggest regret is the last sentence of the piece where I wrote, "The time has come that, once and for all, Islamic infiltration is finally met with a stern and uncompromising form of American resistance."[64] Now, let my view here be crystalline: I absolutely do not support violence of any kind. Certainly not the particularly brutal flavor of violence so often coming from being uncompromising. The resistance I was referring to was cultural, to specifically the understanding that when there is a culture seeking to dominate as opposed to assimilate abroad, that will create tension in society, one to be addressed though however it gets addressed, nonviolently and as agreed upon by society, of course. But once again, I was an ember-hued shade of red in my prose when it should have been colored with a dispassionate gray. *Mea maxima culpa*.

Given the number of this kind of sin I have committed over the years, reference to them must necessarily be rather summary. But I'll press on . . .

That same year, I published another couple of articles with Laura, this time concerning a local controversy that garnered national attention and even a series of kind tweets from then-President Trump.

In the neighboring town of Saint Louis Park in Minnesota where I lived at the time, there was a sensational kerfuffle about the removal of the Pledge of Allegiance from the agenda of its city council which previously began every session.

There were two pieces I penned on the ordeal for which I want to offer my penitence, first on the reporting of the banning and the second (which I covered on-site for Laura Loomer) on its eventual reinstatement.

In the first piece, I reference councilwoman Anne Mavity's apologizing to the city's staff for having to reckon with a call volume far higher than normal, courtesy of outrage regarding the ban. I quote myself from years back when I referred to this apology as a "disgraceful and arrogant act."[65]

I then went on to ask, "Why do the caretakers of local Minnesota government deserve an apology for being forced to do their jobs?"[65] Any reader of this article who would be interested in my disposition while writing might imagine me salivating at the mouth, face reddened with outrage, and anxious to deafen my readers with my vocal setting of eleven.

I then make a separate point, but it's more of a half-point tinged with suggestive allusion that might guide a reader down a dark and gloomy conspiratorial path.

Here is that passage in full:

> A single damning piece of information to note here is that controversial Congresswoman Ilhan Omar was present at a St. Louis Park Council meeting no less than two weeks before the egregious vote to squeeze American sentiment from this entirely American convening. While nothing on the agenda here explicitly states Omar was to

> address the question of the [P]ledge, it seems more than slightly suspect that the notoriously anti-American Omar was present at said meeting prior to the ultimately anti-American decree of banning the [P]ledge of [A]llegiance in their hallowed halls.[65]

Notice how I somewhat contradict myself by admitting, dare I say even asserting, "nothing on the agenda here explicitly states Omar was to address the question of the [P]ledge," and yet that doesn't stop me from pointing, by way of inference, a finger at her as "notoriously anti-American."[65]

Also, to call something *damning* implies conversation-ending evidence. It's the infamous smoking gun. It is, quite simply, matter settling.

A politician going to a political meeting to discuss politics doesn't quite strike me in retrospect as wholly deserving of the designation of *damning*.

I also rather bravely refuse to cite examples of her being anti-American. As a quite relevant aside, some years later, Omar would vote for renewing the Zadroga Act which would grant compensation to first responders who suffered horrific ailments as a result of working at Ground Zero after 9/11.[67] That seems like a fairly American act to me.

From there, I went on a rampage of bad-faith excursions in a third piece I wrote, this time on the reinstatement of the pledge. In this piece I enthusiastically attack (only in print, of course) several members of the city council.

Beginning with my warm and tender characterization "The council... proceeded to bathe in the steam of self-pity," I gleefully noted "an endless stream of 'why is everyone picking on us' characterized the utterances of almost everyone on the council."[66]

I then proceeded to aim the gun barrel of my prose at Ward Council member Tim Brausen. I referred to him as being in an "advanced" bout of tone-deafness. That right there isn't even a try at stating a fact, let alone a relevant one. That is pure conjecture on offer by a less-than-polite and certainly less-than-timid writer.

Heroically, I then proceeded to double down by fulminating, "Mr. Brausen, in a courageously toxic trifecta of arrogance, fake outrage, and evasion, blubbered about Fox [News Network] themselves not saying the [P]ledge of [A]llegiance before each broadcast."[66]

I'll grant, it is probably fun to read, and it was certainly fun to write. That is precisely the lurid seduction of untempered, on the verge of performative, indignation. (After all, I haven't thought about Mr. Brausen since the piece was published, so how authentic could my indignation have been?)

There is an intoxicating thrill in wielding words as weapons—of course in service to your tribe—such that the satisfaction of the resultant verbal takedown can momentarily eclipse reason or restraint. But one of the many problems with this is online news outlets have a particularly unforgiving memory. Indeed, my scornful remarks live on to this day.

I went on to characterize Mr. Brausen as someone who was not "content to only look foolish once." Perhaps, it's a kind of poetic justice that I now find myself bathing in foolishness as I ruminate on my past misdeeds in these pages.

In any event, he let rip some criticism of news networks that chose to seize upon this "issue" (his use of quotation marks, not mine) in an effort to "divide us all." That was perfectly fair criticism, one I was incapable of reporting without an insufferable air of contempt.

I closed the curtain on Mr. Brausen by remarking how his eventual decision to reinstate the Pledge was a "decent enough action until [he] closed by saying that he only did it so citizens would stop 'complaining about others and how they open their meetings.'" Does that line lean more toward journalism or more toward activism?

After some admittedly warm praise of tearful "Large A" Council member Steve Hallfin, which by the way was only because he made his own string of *mea culpas* to which I would have considered representative of "my side" at the time, I next lined up in my sights, once again, Ward 2 council member Anne Mavity.

First, she called to attention the idea that wearing a flag in any form such as a hat, dress, etc. was itself a desecration of a kind, which is true per flag code[68]. I saw this as a dodge and wasn't at all afraid to inject personal bias, opinion, and—once again—a less than moderate vocal setting into the soiree. I wrote at that time the "vulgar attempt at grandstanding" was "completely irrelevant to the proud tradition of the sacred Pledge," while also showcasing "a resort to sordid euphemism."

If I am being honest, I still don't completely disagree with that sentiment, but once again I came into it with a level of energy I certainly could—in fact *should* have—tempered. Bear in mind, I supposedly presented the visage of a journalist at the meeting, not a passionate citizen. I also tried what I now see as a sleight of hand trick regarding the flag code. Though I cite the code, I made the personal observation—and it was a personal observation—that the code "recommends not wearing the flag as an etiquette guideline, not as a matter of patriotism" and was thus irrelevant. I'll let you decide, dear reader, if there is any level of dishonesty involved there, but it feels to me like there is at least the hint of it.

It is easy to get carried away with venom-soaked prose. Fierce pieces of that kind tend to be quite invigorating to write, particularly for someone like me who may want to (at least at the time) exercise a Hitchensian job on a subject as the one applying the poisoned pen.

Indeed, I was—at my highest ambition—a Hitchens clone creating a polemical masterpiece as he had against the likes of Henry Kissinger and Bill Clinton. Or perhaps the imagined intrepid muckraker I saw myself as was akin to Jessica Mitford taking down the risible Famous Writers School. Regardless, it was hatred—one that was of course in lockstep with my tribe—or at least the simulacrum of hatred that was the great engine fueling much of my work at that time.

Hatred, though it often provides rather junky energy, can be a tremendous way of springing out of bed in the morning and keeping one going. I used to think, *Yes, it's junky. But it IS energy.* Now, a few years down the road with the always beneficial perspective of hindsight as I gaze in the rearview mirror of my life, I would now say, *Yes, it's energy, but it IS junky.*

So, allow me to be the first penitent head to bow, dear readers.

I confess to Almighty God and to you, my brothers and sisters, that I have greatly sinned, in my thoughts and in my words, in what I have done and in what I have failed to do, through my fault, through my fault, through my most grievous fault.

These are of course only a partial rendering of my sins, among a plethora of others, I assure you.

So, those are some of my sins. What are some of yours?

CHAPTER 13

The Way Out

First, I want to jump in front of an anticipated criticism and, as Buckley would say, stand "athwart" it to yell "stop."

Even as I write, I can already hear the distant echoes of readers who might feel compelled to call me on what seems to be a paradox in my prose.

"Cohen, you have written a book ostensibly aimed at addressing tribalism in our day and to, however minimally, clean up the devastation wrought by the debt of vitriol that tribalism incurs, and yet you seem to criticize leftism in a more barbed and frequent way than you critique the Right," the imagined cartoon of a critic in my mind scoffs.

It's a fair criticism, but I have a more-than-fair rebuttal, at least in my view. It happens to be the case that the great or at least once-great institutions of our day have been uniquely captured by the Left in a way the Right just hasn't. To simply notice this is not my fault.

It's not just that Left-leaning institutions deserve pointed criticism; it's that all institutions, whether leaning Left or Right, must be held accountable when they drift into ideological rigidity. Buckley understood this well, and his scathing rebukes of the John Birch Society and George Wallace are proof that no ideological tribe, including his own, was immune to his scrutiny.

The issue today is, the right-wing institutions simply don't dominate the spaces where these battles are most urgent. Academia, mainstream media, and the cultural behemoths of Hollywood and Big Tech are overwhelmingly influenced by leftist orthodoxy. This is not an ideological gripe but an observation about the imbalance of power. Criticizing these institutions for their partisanship is not the same as endorsing the partisan excesses of the Right. Buckley's commitment to rigorous debate and ideological diversity would have demanded the same of them.

In short, there simply isn't as much meat to chomp through with regard to criticism of institutions that have been captured by the Right. I suspect Buckley, with the vitriol he aimed at the JBS and the racist governor of Alabama, would feel the same way, though I am of course as much a slave to speculation as anyone else on that point.

With that perceived imbalance addressed and the stage set, it's time to reflect on the values and principles we've explored throughout this book, tying them together to offer a way forward, in fact, the way out; the way leveraging Buckley's vision of principled engagement, dialogue, and the pursuit of a more unified, less polarized society

Decency & Humor

Evil and darkness, dear reader, will most readily and effectively descend into our culture when we all stop talking to each other. That is perhaps the dirtiest deed wrought by tribalism in the culture today. With everyone siloed in their respective echo chambers, that allows misinformation to fester, and fear to breed. When dialogue is abandoned, nuance is lost, and understanding gives way to hostility. In this atmosphere, the seeds of division are sown, creating a landscape where empathy is overshadowed by animosity.

Few have done more to promote debate and dialogue than the host of the immortal *Firing Line* and the happy warrior through countless debates, William F. Buckley Jr. A smart man would turn away the challenge to name someone more committed to giving sunlight to opposing ideals. Toxic ideals thrive in darkness and silence, and they are—as we all know—disinfected by the unforgiving light of the sun.

So we must reclaim the art of conversation, engage with those who challenge our views, and listen deeply rather than defensively. Only through this genuine exchange can we hope to bridge the chasms tribalism has carved into our society, fostering a culture where diverse perspectives enrich our collective understanding rather than diminish it. In doing so, we fortify the foundations of democracy, ensuring our shared humanity prevails over the allure of divisive rhetoric.

One of the other great tragedies of ideological siloing and political deformities is the unrestrained alacrity with which the opposing side is represented.

In discussion, one is either striving to understand the opposing side or striving to *mis*understand the opposing side. Take immigration, for example. Individuals and institutions alike—who are determined to ascribe the lowest possible motives to those opposed to illegal immigration—would struggle with, this time, a series of political-flavored Rorschach tests.

They would, by their own hand and no one else's see the opposition and translate it into racism, or American exceptionalism, or some bizarre form of white supremacy, whereas others will look at it and simply see the self-evident problems of keeping a healthy democracy and border security.

This kind of misrepresentation isn't just wrong; it's destructive. When we refuse to engage with the complexities of opposing arguments, when we pigeonhole people into caricatures, we not only alienate potential allies but also deepen the divides in our society. Buckley, with his commitment to dialogue, was acutely aware of this danger. His long history of debating adversaries, often in adversarial and highly public forums, shows he believed in confronting ideas, not caricatures.

These caricatures can very much take on life in the community—to devastating effects. In October 2024, when America was in the throes of a historic election, this came to bear in Alabama.

A Birmingham Baptist church, New Era Baptist, sparked justifiable controversy with a sign targeting Black voters who planned to vote for Trump. The sign, posted by Pastor Michael Jordan, read, "Attention to all blacks who plan to vote for Trump, you are an ignorant stupid negro," and on the reverse side, "Warning African Americans: A vote for Trump will put Blacks back to picking cotton."[69] Jordan, who at the time had led the church for thirty-two years, said his role as pastor compels him to speak out, calling it his "ministry" and "calling." So, he committed this egregious act of racism with, as C. S. Lewis put it, "the permission of his own conscience."

This isn't the first time Jordan's signs have generated attention. Ahead of the 2020 election, another sign displayed, "A black vote for Trump is mental illness" and "A white vote for Trump is pure racism."[69] To no one's great surprise, local Trump supporters criticized the sign, arguing it created a hostile environment for worshippers.

Despite the backlash, Pastor Jordan defended his stance, saying God motivates him to stand for what he believes is right. He encouraged critics to "read the Bible and look in the White House" if they questioned his views. The sign has drawn further condemnation from Alabama Lt. Gov. Will Ainsworth, who accused it of threatening, intimidating, and insulting voters. Not exactly a masterclass in understanding the other side and certainly not a profile in decency.

The willingness to engage with ideas in a substantive way is critical to healthy public discourse. For Buckley, debate was the lifeblood of democracy. It's something we have forgotten as we've allowed our tribes to define the terms of engagement, reducing all differences into binary choices and leaving no room for complexity or nuance which is virtually always where the truth lives.

But there is far more to the way out than simply being willing to talk and debate, though there is that.

The hypertribalism we find ourselves in really is tearing at the fabric of our society. At the time of this writing, there is a nasty presidential campaign being waged by Trump and Kamala Harris. The sole or at least the salient goal of both of these campaigns has been to demonize the other candidate and, by extension and inference, those who support them.

The week before the election, it was shown—in a report that can't quite be called revealing or novel—voters are viewing the other side with increasing animus. This in the immediate aftermath of a comedian at a Trump rally now infamously joking that Puerto Rico was an "island of garbage," which led to then-President Biden much less jokingly referring to Trump supporters as "garbage," but more on that momentarily.

"I would say some [Trump supporters] are garbage," said Samantha Leister, thirty-two years old, who ventured to a Kamala Harris rally in, appropriately enough, Harrisburg, Pennsylvania.

Even better than that, Leister went on to say that her Trump-supporting parents as well as her father-in-law are simply "misguided." It was apparently not enough to simply understand the United States is a big country . . . with lots of people… with lots of different priorities . . . who just may view the best way forward through a different lens. The only acceptable enclosing brackets between which they were allowed to disagree with Leister is if they are "misguided."[70]

But that attitude and lack of decency is by no means relegated to the Left.

That same day, Trump was holding a rally in Green Bay, Wisconsin.

Citizen Shawn Vanderheyden had his own tender sweet nothings on offer for Harris supporters.

"I just think they are uneducated, and they believe all the lies," he explained. "It's unfortunate."

But hoping the rest of the country could see that solution through Mr. Vanderheyden's own myopic lens, he kindly admitted he earnestly wishes, "Hopefully [Harris supporters] open their eyes."[70]

One could accuse these examples of simply being anecdotal, and I'll admit that is a tough argument to beat. So, let's examine something a little harder-headed.

Let's turn to a Pew Research poll conducted in the not-so-distant past of late 2022.

Most glaringly, the study found Democrats and Republicans are increasingly inclined to perceive members of the opposing party as lacking intelligence and being lazy, immoral, or dishonest. This might not be particularly surprising, but consider it actually should surprise. Once again, we should be able to disagree without being disagreeable.

After all, if William F. Buckley Jr., the great right-wing icon and maker of the movement was able to do it with his own flavor of love and decency, it seems to me no one else really has much of an excuse.

Just for one point of contact, the study found that back in 2016, 47 percent of Republicans, along with 35 percent of Democrats viewed the opposing party as more immoral. Not great stuff, but OK.

But in 2024, a staggering 72 percent of the GOP as well as 63 percent of Democrats hold the same view.

It gets worse.

The study found, bleakly, in 2024, 72 percent of Republicans and 64 percent of Democrats viewed the other side as more dishonest. It was fewer than half of each party only six years ago.

Pew Research found in terms of what the study called "closed-mindedness" a startling 83 percent of Democrats as well as 69 percent of Republicans see the other side as more closed-minded.[71]

One last point of contact to depress you with, and this speaks perhaps most clearly to the problem of tribalism in our day.

This has to do not just with the problem of disagreement (which really isn't a problem or at least shouldn't be in a country of 300 million people) but to the perception of the actual "harm" being done to the country by the policies of the other.

A considerable portion of Republicans sees their identification with the GOP as a safeguard against the perceived dangers of Democratic policies; 78 percent of Republicans indicate these perceived harms are a significant factor in their party affiliation.

Among Democrats, this sentiment is mirrored, with 68 percent citing the damage they believe Republican policies inflict on the country as a primary reason for their alignment. Both sides, then, are increasingly motivated not merely by policy support but by a sense of needing to counteract what they see as threats posed by the other.

These numbers don't exactly inspire confidence when it comes to making friends with the other side in modern times.

A bit—perhaps more than a bit—of peacemaking is the antidote to all this tribal chaos.

If we have not exhausted the wisdom of the Bible's verses here, Romans 12:18 adds, "If it is possible, as far as it depends on you, live at peace with everyone." [Bible - 16]

Buckley's lessons, shown in both deed and words, just may be the best prescription for the way out of this.

We should all aspire—as Schlesinger accused Buckley of all those years ago—to excess amounts of decency. Be the sort of person whose liberal (pardon the term!) application of decency is so ubiquitous that you, too, will be recognized for it, perhaps even in print. Jeet Heer wrote of Buckley's "basic decency" and his "life-long capacity to change, adapt, and learn." Hendrik Hertzberg noted, Buckley "could not have been happy with the vulgarity of the movement he did so much to spawn." Rick Perlstein described him as "a good and decent man" who honored his ideological adversaries without masking their adversarial nature in false bonhomie. In a time marked by sharp divisions, Buckley's decency remains a model worth striving for, reminding us true conviction is as much about integrity as it is about ideology.

Walking in decency is the first step to climbing out of the social sludge of hypertribalism we find ourselves in. It allows us to see other people—the other side, if you insist—as people. We ought not to be rounded up and shot as the Kansas professor so brazenly suggested. Nor should we judge those who choose to take up a different political mantle.

Now, yes, of course there is a sort of moral critical mass one hits after a perpetual confrontation with toxic ideals. (Remember that moral trip wire?) The toxic ideals are still very much at play, but they should not blind us to the humanity of those we oppose. Recognizing the inherent dignity in others—even when we vehemently disagree with their views—requires a commitment to decency transcending political divides. This doesn't mean we shy away from robust debate or overlook the dangers posed by extremist ideologies.

Instead, it calls us to engage thoughtfully and compassionately, challenging ideas without dehumanizing the individuals who hold them.

In the spirit of such engagement, consider once again how Buckley once jokingly gifted that donkey to Arthur Schlesinger—a playful but profound gesture encapsulating the essence of recognizing our opponents as fully human. Even in jest, such acts of decency reflect the willingness to transcend animosity and engage with one another in a spirit of goodwill.

In a time when polarization breeds contempt, our ability to walk in decency becomes a radical act. It allows us to navigate the complexities of our differences while fostering an environment where dialogue is possible. Buckley understood this deeply: his friendships with those he disagreed with serve as a testament to the power of respectful engagement. By embracing decency, we can begin to rebuild trust, cultivate understanding, and ultimately forge a path toward a more civil society—one where differences are not just tolerated but seen as opportunities for growth.

That is a perfect one-two punch of decency and humor that we need a steady treatment of in our society.

We have forgotten how to recognize a joke, let alone take a joke.

We as a culture also have a morally mandated need to breathe new life into the comedic body of our culture. We have to rediscover our humor.

George Orwell once wrote, "Political chaos is connected with the decay of language."

There was a descent into the depths of decay at that Trump rally held at Madison Square Garden in New York in 2024.

At the Trump rally, comedian Tony Hinchcliffe made a controversial joke referring to Puerto Rico as a "floating island of garbage." Now, it certainly is the sort of joke I wouldn't have made. But it's worth bearing in mind, Hinchcliffe might actually be the very best insult comic on the planet, so the fact he might tell an insulting joke ought not to be terribly surprising.

There was outcry from all the predictable corners of the internet and the media, who rather shrewdly referred to Hinchcliffe as a "speaker" at the rally and not as a "comedian" and treated his joke as a statement instead of a joke, which is perhaps a final example of a failed Rorschach test. There might actually be a million examples we could point to.

Buckley was never one to take a joke personally, and that should be an ideal condition to move toward.

When he made that appearance with Woody Allen on his show, Allen made the teasing comment, "Mr. Buckley cannot do a dance that was invented after 1880."[42] Buckley committed the revolutionary act of laughing at the jab and getting on with it.

During that same television appearance, not incidentally, one young woman in the audience asked him if he thought miniskirts were in good taste. "On you, I think they are," Buckley joked.[42] The young woman laughed and there was a general wave of chuckling that ran across the audience. He meant to tell a joke and it was received as such. Once again, one pines for a move toward that as a societal default.

Perhaps an antidote to all this chaos would be to take the good Congressman Crenshaw up on his challenge to try not to offend but try harder not to be offended. If that was observed by our greater society, we could move forward.

Truth-Seeking As a Glorious Adventure

Another crucial element of walking toward the light—the way out of where we find ourselves—is daring to be a seeker of truth. To understand there are right and wrong answers to the question "Is this good or bad?" Seeking truth will give our society a firm moral orientation from which we can proceed. It will have the great benefit of doing away, once and for all, with the ridiculous and solipsistic notion of "my truth,": that is, the truth is a relative concept with no objective basis of being.

No, to understand there is objective reality and, thus, truth, is to recognize we all live in relation to a common reality upon which our understandings can converge providing we're looking in the same direction and have the same moral tool kit, which we will, by and large.

To lose a sense of objective truth and reality is to lose the platform on which you can reasonably communicate with anyone or have anyone communicate with you.

I suspect you can think of your own favorite example of how even having a base commitment to an objective, rather than a capricious subjective truth, has wreaked havoc on society.

"We find that in the absence of demonstrable truth," Buckley wrote in *God and Man at Yale*, "the best we can do is to exercise the greatest diligence, humility, insight, intelligence, and industry in trying to arrive at the nearest values to truth. I hope, of course, to argue convincingly that having done this, we have an inescapable duty to seek to inculcate others with these values."[80]

So, Buckley's societal prescription would be to seek objective truth, and once attained, one has a moral duty to pass that value on to others.

Here is where things get fun.

There is nothing more adventurous than telling the truth. When you tell the unmitigated truth or at least your closest approximation to it, you simply don't know how it will be taken or what will happen, and thus begins your adventure.

By telling only the truth, you open yourself to an adventure beyond imagining, one where each step unfolds unpredictably, yet you surrender willingly to the unknown.

Truth doesn't just reveal the world; it reveals it as it's meant to be seen. And in embracing this journey, you find yourself swept into the most profound adventure of your life.

There is also a kind of serene wisdom in this ethos: whatever arises from speaking truth is, by its nature, the best reality that could possibly emerge even if its full beauty is hidden at first.

"Let us not love in word or talk but in deed and in truth," 1 John 3:18 directs us. [Bible - 18]

Buckley would—certainly in print and perhaps in policy were he to run and claim finally political office—advocate for a layer of Christian ideals, if not Christian practice to be grafted onto societal psychology.

We must skirt comforting lies in our society in favor of answering the eternal call to adventure, with no adventure having a higher ambition than telling the truth. Buckley's endorsement of Allard Lowenstein is a rather helpful dual lesson of not following lockstep with one's tribe and seeing to its full conclusion, the truth in one's heart.

Buckley would most certainly have written vociferously about the various institutions (some of which he maligned even in his own time) running amok due to tribalism in our society, such as the ACLU and academia in general.

Academia

The institutes of supposed higher learning are often in our day referred to as "indoctrination centers." Indeed, as Colonel North, the dearly departed Dr. Goetsch, and Prof. Jones wrote in their own invective against college campuses that we as Americans have a moral duty and adventure ahead of us in helping "our children avoid poisonous anti-Christian indoctrination they face in everyday life."[81] Buckley spelled this out himself in *God and Man at Yale*.

To be clear, this is by no means an advocacy of theocracy—perish the thought. To the contrary, it's an admonishment to allow all ideals to be tested against not only logic but also reality—and tested at scale. If we view the, so to speak, ideological landscape as not the oft-mentioned marketplace of ideals, but as a hard-fighting battleground of ideals where that disinfecting sunlight becomes so important, then Buckley would no doubt offer Christianity and its ideals up to the most vigorous and unkind scrutiny: he would only ask that it got its fair shot.

But the nonsense we have seen on college campuses, for instance, has not only the blocked disinfecting spotlight of Christianity but drastically dimmed its brightness where wokeness is concerned.

One may instance the salient case of Claudine Gay.

It was January 2 of 2024, when Harvard's thirtieth president, Claudine Gay, announced her resignation. This move, widely regarded as a long time coming, followed months of turmoil during which Gay, newly appointed to her post, made headlines for remaining conspicuously silent when Harvard's student groups lauded brutal attacks in Israel, casting a shadow over Harvard's Jewish community and offering little to no assurance of the institution's support.

In December 2023, Gay faced national scrutiny when testifying before Congress alongside other university presidents, attempting to defend calls for violence as "context-dependent" free speech. Her stance received swift public rebuke, and her reputation was dealt a further blow when reports surfaced accusing her of extensive plagiarism in her doctoral dissertation and published articles. Yet, despite these mounting controversies and clear ethical breaches, Harvard's board stood behind her, seeming more committed to her DEI agenda than to academic integrity.

Why such loyalty? Gay, a vocal proponent of DEI, championed "antiracist" policies aimed at dismantling what she termed "white supremacy"—the "second pandemic"—at Harvard, proposing radical changes in admissions, curricula, and even art to reflect these priorities. For the Harvard Corporation, Gay's ideological fervor aligned with a new vision for the university. But as allegations of academic misconduct and her complicity with antisemitism drew international ridicule, it was clear her leadership had eroded the prestige Harvard once enjoyed.

Following an intervention by board chair Penny Pritzker, Gay stepped down—but with her $900,000 salary and a tenured position intact. DEI advocates, meanwhile, predictably cast her dismissal as an act of racism, arguing she was "trapped" by conservative malice, whatever that means. Such defenses, however, only drew attention to the absurdity of Gay's legacy, which, in its drift from traditional academic standards, epitomizes the moral debt that "woke" leadership incurs. This is no small story but a symbol of the larger rift in academia: the fight between preserving values rooted in rigorous scholarship and, the alternative, abandoning them to ideological fervor.[82]

If anything, the fallout from Gay's resignation reveals just how far today's institutions of higher learning have drifted from ideals of open inquiry and honest debate in favor of an agenda, cloaked in the guise of "equity" and surrendering truth. This is the perfect encapsulation of the dangers on offer from a societal commitment to the toxic ideal of wokeism and all it might imply.

So, once again, we have seen how ideological bias and tribalism have crept into academic settings, restricting the flow of ideas and fostering a culture of self-censorship. But they need not be quite that dramatic or far-reaching.

Whether we are referring to the professor at Los Angeles City College who labeled a student "fascist" simply for his support of traditional marriage or if we remind ourselves of Professor Phillip Lowcock's extreme remarks at the University of Kansas, incidents like these exemplify how academia's intellectual rigor is increasingly compromised by personal political agendas.

These incidents aren't isolated but are part of a larger trend in academia that sidelines open inquiry in favor of echo chambers. Such environments allow figures like Douglas Murray to be met with irrelevant dismissals of historical thinkers—such as Immanuel Kant, to say nothing of God and Christ—for their supposed personal flaws rather than engaging with their contributions to Western thought. These examples remind us of the dangers when academia abandons its commitment to free expression and intellectual honesty.

The path to repatriation would be paved with a willingness to fend off via sensible criticism and debate the toxic ideals running rampant in academia.

Ultimately, the antidote lies—as Buckley would no doubt have argued—in preserving a battleground of ideas where debate is not only allowed but encouraged and where the impulse to dismiss and censor is curbed. Without this commitment, we risk a decline not only in intellectual standards but also in the core democratic values that enable genuine dialogue.

Fanaticism and Partisan Institutions

It seems a cruel irony that in an environment as hypertribalized as ours, the calls to bring down the temperature or tone down the rhetoric would not only fall on deaf ears but also seem to tempt so much of society in the opposite direction. The very notion of dialing back the intensity of our discourse is often dismissed as weak, as if any attempt to temper extremism is a denial of one's commitment to truth. Yet it is precisely in such a polarized atmosphere we need those calls more than ever. When fanaticism becomes the lens through which we view the world, the ability to engage with others in good faith is lost, and the space for reasoned dialogue diminishes.

With that aside and done with, these institutions, with their obvious partisanship, have contributed immeasurably to that vitriol, which is why they appear so prominently. From the demonization of anyone to the right of Buzzfeed in the world of journalism to the aspersions cast at those like Maajid Nawaz who might turn a critical eye to ideologies, it has become taboo to criticize.

I firmly believe no institution is beyond criticism—especially pointed criticism. Any organization positioning itself as above reproach, by its very nature, invites rigorous and often harsh scrutiny from those who are unafraid to speak out. That is when the critics are most justly warranted. All it takes for wickedness to thrive is for good men to do nothing.

The calls for civility are not about diluting our convictions but about steering away from the temptation to view every disagreement as a moral battle demanding total victory or complete annihilation no matter how much blood, metaphorical or otherwise, be spilled. In a time when extremes are valorized, the antidote is not silence but measured discourse creating an environment where ideas are tested not by the fervor of their proponents but by their merit. By dialing down the fanaticism, we allow for a more thoughtful exchange, where the goal is not to destroy the other side but to understand, to challenge, and ultimately to find common ground.

This is not catchpenny drama, though I wish it were.

In late 2024, after much of Florida was ravaged by Hurricane Milton, there was, of course, the cleanup and aid on offer from FEMA (Federal Emergency Management Agency). The organization, which is an agency of the Department of Homeland Security, says plainly and simply its stated goal is "to help people before, during and after disasters."[83] In other words, not something to be politicized, at least in a healthy society.

The poisoned well of fanaticism may have overflowed, then, when a FEMA official directed workers assisting survivors of Hurricane Milton in Lake Placid, Florida, to avoid homes displaying yard signs supporting then-President-elect Donald Trump.

Marn'i Washington, the disaster survivor assistance crew leader for Highlands County, allegedly (at least at the time of this writing) instructed her team not to approach these homes, effectively bypassing them in the course of delivering aid. It's reported that around twenty homes in the area went without door-to-door assistance because of this directive.

According to reports, the guidance to avoid homes with Trump signs or flags persisted from late October through November, with workers leaving notes in the government system stating: "Trump sign no entry per leadership." This politically charged instruction placed unnecessary barriers between survivors and the assistance they needed.[84]

John Holbrook, the long-serving mayor of Lake Placid, expressed shock at the actions, calling it an unacceptable failure of basic human decency in a time of crisis. He emphasized the necessity of coming together to help all community members regardless of political beliefs, especially given the widespread damage the town endured, including destroyed mobile homes and other significant property loss. Holbrook reiterated local relief efforts in Lake Placid were moving forward without any form of political discrimination. In the spirit of fairness, let's acknowledge FEMA did fire Marn'i Washington, but one can't help but intuit this was more of an exercise in face saving.

This seems a case worth lingering on since it makes the point that an excess and careless application of fanaticism can have a real and true human cost. The depression mounts when it seems this isn't the work of one rogue crew leader but, according to Washington, was a common practice.

In the days following her dismissal, Washington spoke out, asserting her directive to skip homes with Trump signs was not an isolated decision. She claimed she was following an unofficial but longstanding FEMA policy of "avoidance first, and then de-escalation" when navigating politically charged areas. This "colossal event of avoidance," she argued, was not limited to Florida; similar practices, she said, have occurred in other conservative regions across the Carolinas.[85]

A FEMA official, speaking anonymously, confirmed avoidance strategies are, via a sneaky network of winks, nods, and nudges, quietly endorsed within the agency, often under the guise of prioritizing "under-resourced, marginalized communities." The source added, this policy has for years led FEMA personnel to routinely pass over homes with visible signs of political conservatism. FEMA's stated mission may be to aid *all* in times of crisis, but according to this insider, relief efforts are sometimes reconfigured by unwritten rules placing ideological division above the stated humanitarian goal.

The fallout from these revelations was swift and severe. Congressional Republicans quickly announced plans to investigate FEMA's practices, alleging a politicized agency under the Biden administration. Representative Carlos Gimenez of Florida called FEMA's actions "reprehensible," decrying any denial of aid to Americans in need due to their political affiliations as an unforgivable breach of trust.

FEMA, however, dismissed Washington's claims as baseless, maintaining no such policy exists and emphasizing Washington's directive contravened agency guidelines. Administrator Deanne Criswell released a statement reaffirming FEMA's commitment to serve all Americans, regardless of politics, and pledged to prevent future incidents of discrimination.

If these accusations reveal anything, it's the frightening ease with which even life-saving services can become tools of division. In a society increasingly primed to interpret every action through a partisan and polarized lens, this is the point in cultural degradation when ideological fealty eclipses compassion.

Another example of unchecked rampant fanatics comes to us not from hurricane-ravaged Florida but from sunny California.

In an alarming display of unchecked bias within the classroom, a Moreno Valley Unified School District history teacher was placed on leave after delivering a vitriolic, profanity-ridden lecture attacking Donald Trump the day after the former president won a second term. In a recording of the tirade posted on X, the teacher—whom the district has yet to identify—called Trump a "rapist draft-dodging coward" and claimed Trump embodies some of Hitler's ideals, a shocking accusation to level at the head of state.

The teacher went further, using inflammatory language to malign Black and Latino voters, arguing that those who did not support Kamala Harris were biased against her "because she has a vagina and uterus." He added Latino supporters of Trump "want to be white." The incident was disturbing not only for its incendiary content but for the contemptuous tone directed at students who may have held different political views.

The district quickly placed the teacher on administrative leave pending an investigation. A spokesperson for the district expressed disapproval, stating the educator's behavior was unacceptable and far from the professional conduct expected in a school setting. The district emphasized its mission to foster a respectful and inclusive environment especially during a time of intense political tension.

Despite the blatant impropriety, the teacher has attracted vocal defenders. A petition on Change.org to reinstate him, referred to by some students as Mr. Perez, has already amassed over 1,200 signatures, with some arguing that the lecture's tone, though extreme, reflected his usual style. "I know it was very strong toned, but that's how he gives his lecture as a professor," said student Mykael James, who was in class during the incident. Another student, Sarah Ghawi, claimed, "It's just devastating to know that they're trying to get him out all because of his opinion."[86]

Unfortunately, a compendium and anthology of fanaticism of this kind could easily fill its own volume, let alone a chapter, showcasing the alarming extent to which extreme ideologies fuel division. This brand of fanaticism thrives on an unyielding desire to annihilate opposing views with little regard for understanding or reconciliation. It prioritizes destruction over dialogue, leaving no room for the humility or grace needed for healing.

Incidents like this demand immediate attention, as unchecked fanaticism in society begins to permeate the spaces meant to be sanctuaries of balanced education. Schools risk becoming arenas for ideological combat rather than spaces for learning where intellectual humility and critical thinking should be paramount. This episode underscores an urgent question for the educational system: where does freedom of speech end and professional responsibility begin?

In an environment not only permitting but celebrating rampant zealotry, classrooms become battlegrounds rather than forums, alienating students and undermining the foundational trust education should uphold. Without firm boundaries and clear standards, we court a future where our schools become hostile echo chambers, incubating intolerance instead of cultivating informed citizens capable of nuanced thought. This fanaticism, left unchecked, will turn the educational system from a place of growth into one of dogma, into an institution mirroring the divisiveness it should seek to cure.

It's a disgraceful example of political fanaticism stepping out of the realm of the intellectual abstract where the benefit of detachment lurks and instead sculpting itself into an emotional manacle that should have weighed on us as society then and should weigh on us still.

Was that commitment to fanaticism stoked by, for instance, then-President Joe Biden when he tweeted , "Donald Trump and MAGA Republicans are a threat to the very soul of this country"?[87] It certainly wasn't discouraged. To sharpen the point, President Biden was saying, in effect, 74 million people who previously voted for Trump are a threat to the "very soul of this country." What would societal acceptance and encouragement of fanaticism be if the president calling half the country a threat to the country doesn't get you there?

This ethic of happy, unapologetic fanaticism has infected supposedly nonpartisan institutions as well.

The SPLC and ACLU

As we saw earlier in the additional cases of organizations like the ACLU and SPLC, fanaticism has a welcome home in mainstream institutions that are supposed to uphold fairness and objectivity. The very institutions that, on paper, exist to safeguard freedoms and promote justice have in some cases embraced a kind of ideological zealotry, seeking to silence or ostracize those with differing views instead of fostering discourse.

Tyler O'Neil, managing editor at *The Daily Signal*, offered a critique of the Southern Poverty Law Center (SPLC) echoing Buckley's own skepticism of ideological overreach. According to O'Neil, the SPLC initially pursued a more than laudable and nonpartisan mission, taking on true hate groups like the Ku Klux Klan and other openly racist organizations. Yet as these targets dwindled (nothing will destroy a campaign quite like success!), O'Neil argued, the SPLC broadened its focus, labeling conservative and Christian organizations—mainstream groups like the Family Research Council (FRC) and Alliance Defending Freedom—as "hate groups" without just cause.

The *Making Hate Pay: The Corruption of the Southern Poverty Law Center* author described the SPLC's evolution, specifically its creation of a "hate map" emerging from the earlier Klan Watch project. Over time, this map shifted from targeting explicit extremists to including socially conservative organizations, effectively equating them with violent hate groups. Such categorization, O'Neil contended, blurred critical distinctions, creating a distorted and damaging narrative.

O'Neil further criticized the SPLC's methods, noting it inflates its count of hate groups by listing individual chapters separately, which artificially boosts the numbers and falsely suggests a rising tide of hate. He pointed to real-world consequences of this approach, referencing a 2012 incident in which an assailant, reportedly influenced by the SPLC's designation of the FRC, attempted a shooting at FRC headquarters.

Further ethical questions, O'Neil noted, arose in 2019, when SPLC cofounder Morris Dees was dismissed following allegations of racial discrimination and sexual harassment. Testimonies from former employees suggest, O'Neil added, the SPLC's focus has shifted toward financial gain over principle, its hate labels serving more as a fundraising tool than a genuine effort to combat hate—a criticism that would likely have resonated with Buckley who had little patience for such ethical lapses.

O'Neil also observed the SPLC's sway on policy: government agencies, including the FBI and the Biden administration, have sometimes relied on its reports. O'Neil pointed to lawsuits, such as the one brought by the Dustin Inman Society alleging defamation, as evidence the SPLC's practices are drawing increased scrutiny.

So the SPLC has a grand tradition of intolerance of which it can be proud.

For O'Neil, the SPLC's practices necessitate public skepticism. Buckley might have urged readers to look carefully beyond moralistic claims, recognizing how misapplied labels can undermine civil discourse and skew public understanding.[55]

The ACLU, once a champion of free speech, has in certain instances traded its commitment to open dialogue for ideological purity, much as the SPLC, a civil rights organization, has been criticized for wielding its credibility in a way that targets ideological opponents rather than fostering the unity it once sought to uphold. This transition from institutions grounded in the defense of truth to ones entangled in the machinery of political dogmatism is a troubling manifestation of the very fanaticism that has bled into society at large.

The point here is, fanaticism has infected not only the average person, which would be bad enough, but is currently being championed by the highest offices of our society, up to and including our previous commander-in-chief.

A society grounded in fanaticism will fracture because it demands loyalty not to truth or reason but to rigid ideologies, leaving no room for nuance. William F. Buckley Jr. understood this deeply. He navigated the intellectual landscape of the mid-20th century by rejecting the extremes of both the far-left and far-right, advocating instead for a conservatism rooted in reason, openness, and a commitment to dialogue.

Buckley believed true conservatism was never about blindly adhering to rigid dogma but about engaging with ideas in a way that tempered fervor with respect for the individual.

His rejection of ideological purity was not a call for intellectual dilution but a reminder of how intellectual strength is found in the willingness to engage, question, and ultimately disagree without resorting to the tactics of demonization. That is the winning recipe for disagreeing without being disagreeable.

Only by reining in the excesses of our rhetoric and tempering the fervor fueling our tribal instincts can we hope to preserve the space for authentic dialogue and mutual respect. In Buckley's view, true strength lies not in the ability to overwhelm one's opponents but in the capacity to disagree without demonizing, to listen without surrendering, and to build a society that values the exchange of ideas over the impulse to destroy those with whom we disagree.

For Buckley, this was not just an ideal for public discourse. It was essential for preserving the bonds holding society together in times of deep division, and the pole of that is readily on display for those who care to look.

Journalism

In a time when the media increasingly serves as a mouthpiece for partisan narratives, Buckley's journalistic vision stands as an antidote to the distortion and selective reporting that has become the norm. In the case of Joe Biden, we see a troubling pattern where the media seemed more concerned with protecting his image than with reporting the truth. Biden's mental lapses, that became undeniable to anyone paying attention, are still being downplayed or outright ignored. Whether it's a muddled sentence, a lapse in memory, or an apparent misjudgment, the media bent over backward to avoid confronting the reality of his condition. This is not a new phenomenon in the age of hyperpolarization, but it illustrates just how far the press has strayed from its duty to truth.

And in the aftermath of Biden exiting the office, the legacy media have refused to acknowledge their role in the cascade of cover-ups it perpetrated during Biden's time in office. In fact, CNN's Jake Tapper, who happily threw guests off his show for suggesting Biden was mentally gone, now cashes in with his book, *Original*

Sin: President Biden's Decline, Its Cover-Up, and His Disastrous Choice to Run Again, which claims to examine, among other things, Biden's mental fitness—or lack thereof—as if any of it was news to anyone who has been paying attention for the last half decade.

A decent test for partisanship to apply here is to simply ask if the level of scrutiny and attention to obvious mental lapses would have been the same if a Republican—Trump, for instance—were in office. In fact, I think I remember some journalists/pundits making accusations about Trump's lack of mental and physical acuity when Biden came under scrutiny.

The press, instead of asking hard questions, too often shields political figures from examination. This is a far cry from Buckley's vision of journalism. For Buckley, journalism was not about protecting the powerful or ignoring uncomfortable realities; it was about confronting them head-on. Journalism, in his eyes, should be a constant search for the truth no matter where it leads. In today's world, where the media often refuses to challenge its own ideological predispositions, Buckley's commitment to intellectual honesty is more important than ever.

Take, for example, how the media's refusal to acknowledge Biden's lapses mirrors a larger trend of media dishonesty. The mainstream press has become a place where facts are manipulated to maintain ideological purity, where truth is sacrificed on the altar of political allegiance. The result is a world where the lines between fact and opinion are increasingly blurred, where the media's primary function is not to inform but to reinforce the narratives of the tribe.

Buckley's approach to journalism was different. When he founded *National Review*, it wasn't just to give a platform to conservative viewpoints: it was to engage with the full range of ideas, testing them through reason and debate. Buckley rejected the idea that journalism should be mere cheerleading for one side of the political spectrum. Instead, he embraced the role of the journalist as a truth-seeker, one who could engage opposing viewpoints and subject them to scrutiny not out of a desire to win but out of a commitment to uncovering the deeper truths beneath the surface.

In today's fractured media environment, this approach feels revolutionary. The idea of journalists as truth-seekers seems almost quaint given the media's role in amplifying division and feeding tribal instincts. But Buckley's model still holds weight, especially when we see the lengths to which the media will go to shield its political allies from criticism. Journalism, as Buckley understood it, should never be about simply pushing a particular narrative or ideologically driven agenda. It should be about the search for truth even when truth is uncomfortable or inconvenient.

In Buckley's time, when mainstream outlets were largely liberal, *National Review* was a beacon of intellectual honesty and engagement. He understood, in a democracy, journalism must serve to inform the public, to challenge assumptions, and to present the facts—not through the lens of ideology but through the lens of reason and fairness. Buckley's editorial vision was clear: he wanted to foster an environment where ideas could be debated seriously, where opposing viewpoints were not demonized, and where the search for truth was paramount.

The media's treatment of Biden's cognitive state is a perfect example of why Buckley's approach remains crucial today. When the media refuses to engage with the facts, when it downplays or flat-out ignores uncomfortable truths, it betrays the public trust. In this case, the media's refusal to acknowledge Biden's lapses doesn't just protect the Democrat party. It undermines the public's ability to make informed decisions. It creates a world where political figures are treated as infallible and where the truth is obscured by a veil of convenience and denial.

In contrast, Buckley's legacy challenges us to push past the ideological comfort zones we've built for ourselves and to engage with the world as it is. Journalism, in Buckley's view, was about more than just telling people what they wanted to hear; it was about confronting those uncomfortable truths happily and head-on, engaging with them thoughtfully. Today, in an era when media outlets have become more concerned with keeping their ideological tribes satisfied than with upholding journalistic integrity, Buckley's model serves as a necessary reminder of what is at stake.

The real test for journalists today is not merely to report the news but to report the truth—especially when the truth is inconvenient or politically unpalatable. Journalism should not be a tool for partisan warfare or ideological purity. It should be a tool for uncovering the facts, for fostering genuine debate, and for challenging the assumptions governing our political and social lives.

Buckley's approach was never about hiding from controversy; it was about engaging with it no matter how difficult or divisive doing so might be. In the case of Biden's mental lapses, the media's failure to engage with the truth reflects the larger problem of journalistic dishonesty—a problem Buckley would have recognized all too well.

The problem of "fixing" journalism is a cultural conundrum requiring maximal effort from the industry itself. The doors out of that particular flavor of dishonesty will not get opened from the outside; they will get bashed apart from the inside. The modern information ecosystem is not currently optimizing for truth. It's optimizing for outrage, fanaticism, and the particular flavor of engagement those traits produce.

But the first step needs to be recognizing the issue and the level of toxicity that sort of dishonesty has reached. The media's, may I say, cover-up of America's then-president's mental state can be the first, last, and final showing of the need for repatriation within the fifth estate.

Forgiveness

In the spirit of moving forward as a nation, as a culture, we have to embrace the grand Christian virtue of forgiveness. We all endeavor to live in a society where we are allowed to seek forgiveness and where we are forgiven. This is the charming dialectic that will maximize well-being as a culture.

There is a stunning lack of grace currently engulfing our culture where we seem intent on judging people (of course particularly those who live in other tribes) and defining people by their worst moment or cherry-picking some particular grievance about them that leaves no room for understanding or forgiveness. This impulse to judge others by isolated mistakes or a single flaw fosters a cycle of relentless criticism where empathy and the possibility of growth are discarded in favor of outrage. In such a climate, true grace—the ability to see beyond a person's imperfections and recognize their potential for change—is stifled. Instead, we need a culture that values forgiveness, one that allows us to engage with others in their entirety rather than reducing them to a list of grievances or transgressions.

People make mistakes which are often given unforgiving amplification by social media. Best of all, these mistakes or statements are almost always on offer without context. So we don't even have a proper picture of the circumstances, yet we leap so quickly to judge.

One couldn't think of a better example than Buckley's forgiveness, by deed if not by word, of Whittaker Chambers. It is worth a moment's pause and reflection on the idea that a Soviet spy who ran a network of like-minded spies within the United States and was running information back to the Kremlin could conceivably saunter to Buckley's good side. Yes, Chambers certainly exhibited a form of penitence by pointing to Alger Hiss, among others, but the strength of character Buckley showed in welcoming Chambers to his beloved *National Review* can serve as a lesson for the Right and the Left in today's society.

And the Christian virtue of forgiveness is available for immediate export and emulation by even humanists, atheists, secularists. Matthew 6:14–15's sweet and appealing statement "If you forgive other people when they sin against you, your heavenly Father will also forgive you. But if you do not forgive others their sins, your Father will not forgive your sins" [Bible - 19] is fully embraceable by all ideologies.

In fact, it is the full cultural embrace of these values, dear reader, that will navigate our society's Damascus Journey out of the virulent and vitriolic time in which we find ourselves. The proper inoculation to hyperpolarization is heaping doses of decency and grace. We have to reorient our society toward a repudiation of a fanaticism which will, by the nature of that repudiation, guide us back toward moderation. One book of the Bible less likely to be called upon for moral instruction than others is the book of Titus. But Titus 3:10 offers the perfect prescription here: "Warn a divisive person once, and then warn them a second time. After that, have nothing to do with them." [Bible - 20]

Gratitude

It stands as a peculiar oddity of our day that the most scornful and vociferous cultural criticism seems to be uniquely addressed to the West. Less-than-polite opponents never quite seem more exquisitely complacent than when they disdain America and its values. Consider the aforementioned instances of condemning the West for the eternal sin of slavery which did happen, but which has also been true of more or less every culture in the history of the world and which is by no means abolished still in many parts of the world, a rarely acknowledged reality. These critiques often overlook the West's unique strides in confronting and attempting to rectify such injustices.

But because history does love its ironies, appreciation for these achievements seems to be at an all-time low. There are, once again, the chattering ideologues who condemn America as irredeemably racist because we committed the egregious act of slavery. Never mind virtually every society ever existed practiced slavery[103] and never mind America was the first to abolish practiced slavery.

America as a culture has contained within it a communal moral intelligence that we, thanks to the glorious founding documents of our country, are able to apply as a sort of correction mechanism for social redress. It was that moral intelligence that allowed for the abolition of slavery, the success of the civil rights movement, and the ongoing dialogue about freedom of speech and the necessity to defend it. It feels as if we truly don't know how lucky we are to have such a self-correction mechanism at the ready to affect change.

As a relevant aside, one has to notice those who condemn America on charges of a white supremacist foundation, of a patriarchal tyranny, or of being an institute of fascism never actually seem terribly anxious to leave.

This cavernous gulf between the condemnation and the action (or lack thereof) demands to be noticed.

A reorientation toward gratitude, dear reader, should be the clarion call for all Americans on across the entire political spectrum, whether gazing out of that Overton window or standing on the fringes looking in. We need a concerted mobilization of enthusiasm for national service as a token of that gratitude. It would not be mandatory, but to not participate in these programs would incur a social debt. Stigmas can have great utility in society in many ways, despite our culture's general hearty embrace of shamelessness and nonjudgment. When Buckley noted how if Harvard, for instance, embraced national service as a necessary prerequisite for admission, there would be a sort of trickle-down effect, one suspects he would have been right.

But far from an orientation in that way, there are those who do actually seek to destroy America and its founding values and build anew.

In other words, the idea of gratitude has become a foreign concept. Buckley may well have been on to something by insisting on some sort of voluntary social plan encouraging a year of public service. It also would provide Americans, particularly younger ones who seem especially starved for it, with a sense of duty.

Once again, while it would not be a mandatory conscription—that would entirely defeat the purpose—there would be a gentle social stigma imposed on those who chose to not engage in that show of gratitude. In the same way that a college, for instance, might call upon its prospective applicants to have a certain amount of extracurricular activities for consideration, they could also call for that year of civic duty.

All of our words and actions should reflect gratitude, and the program Buckley hands out to us from history speaks to that ethic.

In *The Brothers Karamazov*, Dostoyevsky's devil is entirely numb to the touch of gratitude because only someone intent on running down the road of malintent would be denied its tranquility, either by their own hand or by someone else's.

The devil relays to brother Ivan, "My best emotions, such as gratitude, for example, are formally forbidden me solely on account of my social position."[88] It is worth private reflection—and perhaps public as well—on what the sweet nectar of gratitude might be denied to the devil.

The devil swims in resentment, the opposite of gratitude.

Resentment blinds the devil to the inherent beauty of human connection and the richness that gratitude can bring to life. In a world where entitlement and resentment often stomp out appreciation, Buckley's vision of a year of public service could serve as a powerful antidote, reorienting individuals toward a sense of community and shared purpose.

Imagine young Americans dedicating a year to serve others, discovering firsthand the transformative power of gratitude through acts of kindness and service. This experience would not only foster empathy but also instill a deep understanding of the responsibilities that come with freedom. By embracing such a program, we would create an environment where gratitude is not merely an abstract concept but a lived reality—one permeating our institutions and everyday interactions.

In this light, gratitude becomes that catalyst for change. It compels us to consider our place within a larger tapestry of humanity, where our contributions matter and our connections deepen. The gentle social pressure to participate in acts of service would remind us gratitude is not passive; it demands action and engagement with the world around us.

In his call for a more civil society, Buckley reminds us that cultivating gratitude is essential for building bridges across ideological divides. By fostering a culture that values civic duty and personal responsibility, we can revive the ethic of gratitude Buckley championed, enriching our national discourse and enhancing our lives in the process. Without it, we as a culture incur, as Buckley put it, "a callousness that breeds ugliness of behavior."[22]

It seems we do actually have a rather full ledger of debt to our country, and that balance should be paid. Is there any other time or any other country in all human history you would rather live? Perhaps there is, but given the hard-won cultural awards of equal rights under the law, the acknowledged evils of slavery, the insistence on the primacy on freedom of speech, and the wonderful pluralism that crops up in a society embracing these values, it seems America is, in fact, worth a dip of the flag, a pause, and a salute in gratitude for being able to live within the brackets of those ideals.

The point of this book, a paean to both Buckley and the oft-forgotten, irrevocably Christian virtues of trans-ideological bonding, has been to conscript recruits from both the Left and the Right whose attention to the problem of tribalism stagnated or worse they, such as myself, had taken part. The purpose is to win them not only in the present but to preserve their fealty for the future.

May this book infuse Buckley's spirit, which was inspired and guided by the Holy Spirit, into enough people to enable us to look not at the ashes of a culture divided by tribalism but at the well-planted seeds of hope that can bloom into a glorious future.

Notes

1. John F. Fink, "Bill Buckley: The Most Important Catholic Conservative," *The Criterion*, (Indianapolis: Archdiocese of Indianapolis, 2017), https://www.archindy.org/criterion/local/2017/11-24/fink.html.
2. Matthew Malone, "William F. Buckley Jr., the St. Paul of the Conservative Movement" (WordonFire.org, 2024), https://www.wordonfire.org/articles/william-f-buckley-jr-the-st-paul-of-the-conservative-movement/.
3. William F. Meehan III, ed., *Conversations with William F. Buckley* (Jackson: University Press of Mississippi, 2009), 154.
4. Fr. Daniel Maria Klimek, "William F. Buckley's Little-Known Devotion to Italian Mystic Maria Valtorta" (*ChurchPop.com*, 2016), https://www.churchpop.com/william-f-buckley-devotion-mystic-maria-valtorta/.
5. Rich Lowry, interview by Josh Cohen, unpublished, 2024.
6. *The Incomparable William F. Buckley,* filmmaker Barak Goodman, aired April 5, 2024 on PBS, *pbs.org/american masters.*
7. William F. Buckley Jr., *Nearer, My God: An Autobiography of Faith* (New York: HarperCollins, 1997), 147–160, 277–286.
8. NR Symposium, "WFB's Faith" (*National Review*, 2017), https://www.nationalreview.com/2017/02/william-f-buckley-jr-catholic-church-faith-anniversary-death-symposium/.
9. "Conrad Black on William F. Buckley Jr." (*National Post*, 2008), http://www.nationalpost.com/news/story

.html?id=338957. Replace with this citation for Rusher quote - William A. Rusher, *The Rise of the Right* (Washington, D.C.: National Review, 1993)

10. William F. Buckley Jr., "William F. Buckley Jr. Interview (1968)," *The Memory Hole,* YouTube video, 1968, https://www.youtube.com/watch?v=f0o3JhhOe88&t=2435s.
11. Personal Letter Obtained by Author (WFB/National Review, 1971).
12. The Episcopal Church, *Racial Justice Audit of Episcopal Leadership* (2021), https://www.episcopalchurch.org/ministries/racial-reconciliation/racial-justice-audit/.
13. Douglas Murray, *The War on the West* (London: Bloomsbury, 2022), 188–197, 203–204, 221–223.
14. Maryam Khanum, "Kansas Professor in Trouble After Calling for Men Who Won't Vote for a Woman President to Be Lined Up and Shot," *Latin Times*, October 10, 2024, https://www.latintimes.com/kansas-professor-trouble-after-calling-men-who-wont-vote-woman-president-lined-shot-561835.
15. Christopher Hitchens, *Christopher Hitchens on Gore Vidal and William F. Buckley Jr.*, YouTube video, 2019, https://www.youtube.com/watch?v=T1gEfl6WDTk&t=161s.
16. William F. Buckley Jr., moderator Michael E. Kinsley, et al., *A Firing Line Debate: Resolved: The Federal Government Should Not Impose a Tax on Electronic Commerce*, Episode FLS401, Hoover Institute Library and Archives, Firing Line Broadcast Records (December 3, 1999), https://www.youtube.com/watch?v=DzLD7fGtjyg&t=2534s.
17. Peter Slen, *In Depth with Christopher Hitchens* (C-SPAN, September 2, 2007), https://www.c-span.org/program/in-depth/christopher-hitchens/175798.
18. Christopher Buckley, "Postscript: Christopher Hitchens, 1949-2011," *The New Yorker* (December 15, 2011), https://www.newyorker.com/news/news-desk/postscript-christopher-hitchens-1949-2011.

19. Christopher Hitchens, "A Man of Incessant Labor," *Washington Examiner* (March 10, 2008), https://www.washingtonexaminer.com/magazine/2089378/a-man-of-incessant-labor/.
20. The White House, "Remarks by President Biden Honoring the Legacy of Senator John McCain and the Work We Must Do Together to Strengthen Our Democracy," news release, September 28, 2023, https://bidenwhitehouse.archives.gov/briefing-room/speeches-remarks/2023/09/28/remarks-by-president-biden-honoring-the-legacy-of-senator-john-mccain-and-the-work-we-must-do-together-to-strengthen-our-democracy/.
21. Trump-Vance, "Crooked Joe Biden and the Radical Left Are Attacking American Democracy," news release, December 2, 2023, https://www.donaldjtrump.com/news/d157eaf9-3be1-4a8a-8d1c-40d16c45b116.
22. William F. Buckley, Jr., *Gratitude: Reflections on What We Owe Our Country* (Random House, 1990), back cover.
23. William F. Buckley, Jr., *Booknotes* interview by Brian Lamb, September 24, 1993, https://www.c-span.org/program/book-tv/happy-days-were-here-again/161343.
24. William F. Buckley, Jr., *Miles Gone By: A Literary Autobiography* (Washington, DC: Regnery Publishing, 2004), 318–329, 278–281, 299–317.
25. William F. Buckley, Jr., *Living It Up with National Review: A Memoir* (UNKNO, 2005), 186–190.
26. Murray Kempton, "Up from Liberalism, by William F. Buckley, Jr.," *Commentary* (February 1960), https://www.commentary.org/articles/murray-kempton/up-from-liberalism-by-william-f-buckley-jr/.
27. John Avlon, "Genius for Friendship," *National Review* (June 12, 2013), https://www.nationalreview.com/magazine/2013/07/01/genius-friendship/.
28. William F. Buckley, Jr., *Cruising Speed: A Documentary* (Putnam, January 1, 1971), 183.
29. Murray Kempton, *Rebellions, Perversities, and Main Events* (Crown, March 29, 1994), vii.

30. Barton Swaim, "Murray Kempton at 100," *Washington Examiner*, December 15, 2017, https://www.washingtonexaminer.com/magazine/858008/murray-kempton-at-100/.
31. Douglas Murray, "Things Worth Remembering: William F. Buckley on 'Pushing Old Ladies Around,'" The Free Press, May 5, 2024, https://www.thefp.com/p/douglas-murray-william-f-buckley.
32. Munk Debates, *Mainstream Media Debate*, November 30, 2022, https://munkdebates.com/debates/mainstream-media/.
33. ESPN News Services, "FBI says rope had been in Talladega garage since October; Bubba Wallace not victim of hate crime," *ESPN*, June 23, 2020, https://www.espn.com/racing/nascar/story/_/id/29354447/fbi-says-rope-had-talladega-garage-last-fall-bubba-wallace-not-victim-hate-crime.
34. Alvin S. Felzenberg, "Buckley's Battle with the Birchers Was No Myth," *National Review*, April 23, 2023, https://www.nationalreview.com/2023/04/buckleys-battle-with-the-birchers-was-no-myth/.
35. Anthony Tommasini, "To Make Orchestras More Diverse, End Blind Auditions," *The New York Times*, 2021, https://www.nytimes.com/2020/07/16/arts/music/blind-auditions-orchestras-race.html.
36. *National Alliance for Audition Support*, League of American Orchestras, https://americanorchestras.org/national-alliance-for-audition-support/.
37. Ibram X. Kendi, "Ibram X. Kendi on Why Not Being Racist Is Not Enough," interview by Owen Jones, *The Guardian*, August 14, 2019, https://www.theguardian.com/world/2019/aug/14/ibram-x-kendi-on-why-not-being-racist-is-not-enough#:~:text=%E2%80%9CI%20don't%20think%20people,how%20they%20should%20fight%20racism.
38. Editorial Staff, "Tackling Systemic Racism Requires the System of Science to Change," *Nature*, May 26,

2021, https://www.nature.com/articles/d41586-021-01312-4.

39. Dan Diamond, "Suddenly, Public Health Officials Say Social Justice Matters More Than Social Distance," *Politico*, June 4, 2020, https://www.politico.com/news/magazine/2020/06/04/public-health-protests-301534.
40. Yana Wang, "A Course Originally Called 'The Problem of Whiteness' Returns to Arizona State," *The Washington Post*, November 12, 2015, https://www.washingtonpost.com/news/morning-mix/wp/2015/11/12/a-course-originally-called-the-problem-of-whiteness-returns-to-asu-as-racial-tensions-boil-over-on-campuses/.
41. Monica Davey, "Odd Couple Stages Debate," *Roanoke Times*, April 4, 1990, https://scholar.lib.vt.edu/VA-news/ROA-Times/issues/1990/rt9004/900404/04040470.htm.
42. "Woody Allen and William Buckley," YouTube video, NBC, December 27, 1967, https://www.youtube.com/watch?v=GNErWi_lTig&t=137s.
43. Dan Crenshaw (@DanCrenshawTX), "Good Rule in Life," Twitter (now X), November 4, 2018, https://x.com/dancrenshawtx/status/1059161623842226176.
44. Patrick Reilly, "Comic Andrew Schulz Accuses BAM of Canceling Stand-Up Hours After He Posted Trump Interview," *New York Post*, October 17, 2024. https://nypost.com/2024/10/17/us-news/comic-andrew-schulz-accuses-bam-of-canceling-stand-up-hours-after-he-posted-trump-interview/.
45. Alexander Cothren and Robert Phiddian, "Friday Essay: Is 'Wokeness' Killing Comedy – Or Are Ageing Comedians Crying Wolf?," *The Conversation*, August 15, 2024, https://theconversation.com/friday-essay-is-wokeness-killing-comedy-or-are-ageing-comedians-crying-wolf-234364.
46. Bill Maher, "Wokeness and Common Sense," Facebook, March 4, 2024, https://www.facebook.com/watch/?v=3650772581856773.

47. George McMillan, "Ricky Gervais Tears Into Woke Culture – 'Pathetic Little Stupid F**King c***,'" *GB News*, February 26, 2023, https://www.gbnews.com/entertainment/ricky-gervais-tears-into-woke-culture-pathetic-little-stupid-fking-c/448940
48. Megan Schumann, "Comedy Can Help Change the World, Rutgers Researcher Says," Rutgers University, June 22, 2020, https://comminfo.rutgers.edu/news/comedy-can-help-change-world-rutgers-researcher-says.
49. Ira Glasser, "Ira Glasser Remembers William F. Buckley, Jr.," *HuffPost*, March 12, 2008 (updated May 25, 2011), huffpost.com/entry/ira-glasser-remembers-wil_b_91175.
50. *Chapters 7 and 8* William F. Buckley, Jr., *A Torch Kept Lit: Great Lives of the Twentieth Century,* James Rosen, ed. (New York: Random House, 2018), 244–249, 311–317.
51. Jay Nordlinger, "Bill at the Ballgame," *National Review*, June 26, 2017, https://www.nationalreview.com/corner/bill-ballgame-when-william-f-buckley-jr-went-watch-baseball/.
52. "Project 2025, Explained," American Civil Liberties Union (ACLU), accessed July 29, 2025, https://www.aclu.org/project-2025-explained.
53. Ira Glasser, "Ira Glasser on Free Speech | Real Time with Bill Maher," interview by Bill Maher, *Real Time with Bill Maher*, YouTube video, January 28, 2022, https://www.youtube.com/watch?v=x0Lc5b8Flto.
54. ACLU of Arkansas, "Civil Rights Groups Tell Federal Appeals Court That Protections for Pregnant Workers Cover Abortion Care," news release, September 3, 2024. https://www.aclu.org/press-releases/civil-rights-groups-tell-federal-appeals-court-that-protections-for-pregnant-workers-cover-abortion-care.
55. Tyler O'Neil, "What Went Wrong with the Southern Poverty Law Center?," interview by Mark Guiney, *Heritage Explains*, The Heritage Foundation, https://www

.heritage.org/progressivism/heritage-explains/what-went-wrong-the-southern-poverty-law-center.

56. "Breaking Ground," Southern Poverty Law Center (SPLC), accessed July 29, 2025, https://www.splcenter.org/.
57. George Orwell, *Animal Farm* (London: Secker and Warburg, 1945), 21.
58. *The Book of Common Prayer*, The Archbishops' Council of the Church of England, 2000-2004, http://justus.anglican.org/~ss/commonworship/word/morningbcp.html.
59. David A. Graham, "The Unlabelling of an 'Anti-Muslim Extremist,'" *The Atlantic*, June 18, 2018, https://www.theatlantic.com/politics/archive/2018/06/maajid-nawaz-v-splc/562646/.
60. Whittaker Chambers, *Witness* (Regnery History: December 8, 2014), 741.
61. Carl T. Bogus, *Buckley: William F. Buckley Jr. and the Rise of American Conservatism* (New York: Bloomsbury Press, 2011), 97.
62. Whittaker Chambers, *Odyssey of a Friend: Letters to William F. Buckley, Jr., 1954–1961* (Washington, DC: Regnery Publishing, 1970), 51, 285, 293–294.
63. Whittaker Chambers, "The Left Understands the Left," *National Review*, November 16, 1957, reprinted February 12, 2020, https://www.nationalreview.com/2020/02/national-review-webathon-whittaker-chambers-the-left/.
64. Josh Cohen, "Some Statistics on Islamic Infiltration in the US in 2019," *Loomered*, June 2, 2019, https://loomered.com/2019/06/02/some-statistics-on-islamic-infiltration-in-the-us-in-2019/.
65. Josh Cohen, "Minnesota Patriots Protest Government-Sanctioned 'Pledge Ban,' Trump Shows Solidarity," *Loomered*, July 14, 2019, https://loomered.com/2019/07/14/minnesota-patriots-protest-government-sanctioned-pledge-ban-trump-shows-solidarity/.

66. Josh Cohen, "Citizen Activism Prevails, St. Louis Park Pledge Reinstated in Minnesota," *Loomered*, July 21, 2019, https://loomered.com/2019/07/21/citizen-activism-prevails-st-louis-park-pledge-reinstated/.
67. Daniel Funke, "Rep. Ilhan Omar 'Voted Yes' to 'Provide Further Funding for the 9/11 First Responders Victims Fund' While Sen. Rand Paul 'Voted No,' *PolitiFact*, July 21, 2019, https://www.politifact.com/factchecks/2019/jul/24/facebook-posts/facebook-post-compares-votes-rand-paul-ilhan-omar-/.
68. U.S. Code, 4 U.S. Code § 8 - Respect for Flag, Cornell Law School: Legal Information Institute , August 12, 1998, amended December 23, accessed July 30, 2025, 2024, https://www.law.cornell.edu/uscode/text/4/8.
69. Morgan Music, "Alabama Church Calls Blacks Who Vote for Trump 'Ignorant Stupid N----' Who Will Bring Back Slavery," *LatinTimes*, October 31, 2024, https://www.latintimes.com/church-trump-alabama-racist-slavery-blacks-vote-pastor-michael-jordan-564238.
70. Chris Megerian, Adriana Gomez Licon, and Marc Levy, "Voters View One Another Across Partisan Divide with Increasing Animosity," *Associated Press*, November 1, 2024, https://apnews.com/article/kamala-harris-donald-trump-joe-biden-garbage-5609afd17f176ed88025c8ae78370218.
71. Pew Research, "As Partisan Hostility Grows, Signs of Frustration with the Two-Party System," Pew Research Center, August 9, 2022, https://www.pewresearch.org/politics/2022/08/09/as-partisan-hostility-grows-signs-of-frustration-with-the-two-party-system/.
72. *Sam Harris vs. Jordan Peterson | God, Atheism, The Bible, Jesus - Part 1*, moderated by Bret Weinstein, Pangburn YouTube video, June 23, 2018, https://www.youtube.com/watch?v=jey_CzIOfYE&t=2693s.
73. William F. Buckley, Jr., "What Mr. Bush Left Out," *National Review*, March 18, 2003, https://www.nationalreview.com/2003/03/what-mr-bush-left-out-william-f-buckley-jr/.

74. "President Donald Trump on Charlottesville: You Had Very Fine People, on Both Sides," CNBC YouTube video, August 15, 2017, https://www.youtube.com/watch?v=JmaZR8E12bs.
75. Emma Colton, "Biden Rehashes Debunked Trump Charlottesville Claim in Late-Night DNC Speech," *Fox News*, August 20, 2024, https://www.foxnews.com/politics/biden-rehashes-debunked-trump-charlottesville-claim-late-night-dnc-speech.
76. Arthur M. Schlesinger Jr., "Inside Conservatism Looking Out," *New York Times*, October 4, 1959, https://archive.nytimes.com/www.nytimes.com/books/00/07/16/specials/buckley-liberalism.html?ref=themorningnews.org.
77. William F. Buckley Jr., "The Ivory Tower," *National Review*, April 5, 1958, reprinted October 23, 2017, https://www.nationalreview.com/2017/10/william-f-buckley-jr-arthur-schlesinger-jr-sacco-vanzetti-lies/.
78. Craig A. Lambert, "Famous Friends," *Harvard Magazine (John Harvard's Journal)*. September 1996 - https://harvardmagazine.com/sites/default/files/html/1996/09/jhj.friends.html, accessed July 30, 2025, https://harvardmagazine.com/sites/default/files/html/1996/09/jhj.friends.html.
79. William F. Buckley Jr., "Arthur Schlesinger, R.I.P.," *National Review*, March 2, 2007, https://www.nationalreview.com/2007/03/arthur-schlesinger-rip-william-f-buckley-jr/.
80. William F. Buckley Jr., *God and Man at Yale: The Superstitions of "Academic Freedom"* (Chicago: Henry Regnery Company, 1951), 140.
81. Oliver L. North, David L. Goetsch, and Archie P. Jones, *American Gulags: Marxist Tyranny in Higher Education and What to Do About It* (Fidelis Publishing, May 24, 2023), 29, 99, 125.
82. Peter W. Wood, "Claudine Gay Was the Embodiment of Woke Academia," *The American Conservative*, January

14, 2024, https://www.theamericanconservative.com/downcast-gay/.

83. "How Can FEMA Help?," FEMA, accessed July 30, 2025, https://www.fema.gov/.
84. Jennifer Kveglis, "FEMA Official Fired for Directing Workers to Avoid Homes with Trump Signs, Lake Placid Mayor Reacts," *Fox 13*, November 10, 2024, https://www.fox13news.com/news/mayor-lake-placid-reacts-fema-official-directing-workers-avoid-trump-supporters-homes.
85. Jennie Taer, Josh Christenson, Emily Crane, and Chris Nesi, "FEMA Worker Accused of Telling Staff to Skip Hurricane-Ravaged Trump Homes Claims It Was Common Practice: 'This Is Not Isolated,'" *New York Post*, November 12, 2024, https://nypost.com/2024/11/12/us-news/fema-worker-accused-of-telling-staff-to-skip-hurricane-ravaged-trump-homes-claims-it-was-common-practice-this-is-not-isolated/.
86. Nathan Solis, "After Teacher's Anti-Trump Rant in Classroom, Moreno Valley School District Places Him on Leave," *Los Angeles Times*, November 11, 2024, https://www.latimes.com/california/story/2024-11-11/moreno-valley-teacher-placed-on-leave-after-giving-post-election-rant-on-trump-to-students.
87. Joe Biden (@JoeBiden), "Donald Trump and MAGA Republicans," Twitter (now X), September 1, 2022, https://x.com/JoeBiden/status/1565492666120523778?lang=en.
88. Fyodor Dostoyevsky, *The Brothers Karamazov* (New York: Penguin Classics, 1958), 769.
89. Lee Lescaze, "Friends Bid Farewell to 'A Gentle Tornado,'" *The Washington Post*, March 18, 1980, https://www.washingtonpost.com/archive/local/1980/03/19/friends-bid-farewell-to-a-gentle-tornado/3d5ccaa4-e94e-4f5b-b01c-fdab9e3989e5/.
90. William F. Buckley Jr., *Let Us Talk of Many Things: The Collected Speeches* (Basic Books, 2008 -), 261–262.

91. Jack Fowler, "Cancel Your Own Goddam Subscription," *National Review*, October 2007, https://www.nationalreview.com/corner/cancel-your-own-goddam-subscription/.
92. Alvin S. Felzenberg, *A Man and His Presidents: The Political Odyssey of William F. Buckley Jr.* (New Haven: Yale University Press, 2017), 113–114.
93. Ann Coulter, "William F. Buckley: R.I.P., Enfant Terrible" Townhall, February 27. 2008, https://townhall.com/columnists/anncoulter/2008/02/27/william_f_buckley_rip,_enfant_terrible-.n846466.
94. Mitchell Langbert, *Imbalanced: A Study of Influence at the University of Virginia*, National Association of Scholars, April 2024, https://www.nas.org/storage/app/media/Reports/Imbalanced%20A%20Study%20of%20UVA/Imbalanced_UVA_Study.pdf.
95. Mel Lyman, , "Buckley & Mailer," *New York Avatar* No. 7, August 18, 1968, https://www.trussel.com/lyman/buckley.htm.
96. Kevin M. Schultz, *Buckley and Mailer: The Difficult Friendship That Shaped the Sixties* (New York: W.W. Norton & Company, 2015), 12–30.
97. Godfrey Hodgson, "William F Buckley Jr Dies at 82," *The Guardian*, February 27, 2008, https://www.theguardian.com/world/2008/feb/27/usa2.
98. William F. Buckley, Jr.,, *In Depth: William F. Buckley Jr.*, interview by Brian Lamb, C-SPAN, April 2, 2000, https://www.c-span.org/program/in-depth/william-f-buckley-jr/171803.
99. Roy R. Silver, "Buckley, Senator, Supports Wydler After Buckley, Columnist, Aids Rival," *The New York Times*, September 1, 1976, https://www.nytimes.com/1976/09/01/archives/buckley-senator-supports-wydler-after-buckley-columnist-aids-rival.html.
100. Charles C. W. Cooke, "*WSJ*: The Conspiracy to Hide Biden's Condition Is Nearly Three Years Old," *National Review*, July 22, 2024, https://www.nationalreview

.com/corner/wsj-the-conspiracy-to-hide-bidens-condition-is-nearly-three-years-old/.

101. John Mulholland, "Inside the White House Cover-Up of Biden's Health Crisis," *The Daily Beast*, August 23, 2024, updated May 13, 2025, https://www.thedailybeast.com/why-did-the-media-stay-so-silent-about-joe-bidens-health.
102. Stef W. Knight, "Inside Biden's Media Evasion," *Axios*, July 3, 2024, https://www.axios.com/2024/07/04/inside-biden-s-media-evasion-sneak-peek.
103. The Editors of Encyclopaedia Britannica, "Slave Trade," last updated June 18, 2025, https://www.britannica.com/topic/slave-trade#:~:text=In%20the%2017th%20and%2018th,illegally)%20into%20the%2021st%20century.